CONFRONTING ILLIBERALISM

A Canadian Perspective

Illiberalism and liberalism compete for the attention of Canadians today. The latter honours values and features that we associate with Western democracies, particularly their democratic institutions and politics, established freedoms, equality of opportunity, and market economies. Illiberal voices challenging them have become more prominent in our politics, universities, and schools and in public administration generally. These voices disparage historical understandings of Western democracy and seek to fundamentally alter its features and values.

In *Confronting Illiberalism*, Peter MacKinnon argues that the liberalism that has been a foundation of Canadian democracy is in decline, resulting in diminished freedom of expression, a deteriorating political and policy environment, and fraying social cohesion. The book investigates claims that are made in the name of freedom, the decline of our politics, the increase of hate crimes, the persistence of inequality, and the vulnerability of our institutions. *Confronting Illiberalism* calls upon Canadians to challenge and resist illiberal influence and to restore liberalism to a central place in our public lives.

PETER MACKINNON is president emeritus of the University of Saskatchewan, an officer of the Order of Canada, and a senior fellow of the Macdonald-Laurier Institute.

UTP insights

UTP Insights is an innovative collection of brief books offering accessible introductions to the ideas that shape our world. Each volume in the series focuses on a contemporary issue, offering a fresh perspective anchored in scholarship. Spanning a broad range of disciplines in the social sciences and humanities, the books in the UTP Insights series contribute to public discourse and debate and provide a valuable resource for instructors and students.

For a list of the books published in this series, see page 121.

CONFRONTING ILLIBERALISM

A Canadian Perspective

Peter MacKinnon

UNIVERSITY OF TORONTO PRESS
Toronto Buffalo London

© University of Toronto Press 2025
Toronto Buffalo London
utorontopress.com
Printed in Canada

ISBN 978-1-4875-6115-4 (paper)   ISBN 978-1-4875-6117-8 (EPUB)
                                      ISBN 978-1-4875-6116-1 (PDF)

Library and Archives Canada Cataloguing in Publication

Title: Confronting illiberalism : a Canadian perspective / Peter MacKinnon.
Names: MacKinnon, Peter, author.
Series: UTP insights.
Description: Series statement: UTP insights | Includes bibliographical references
    and index.
Identifiers: Canadiana (print) 20240390806 | Canadiana (ebook) 20240390857 |
    ISBN 9781487561154 (paper) | ISBN 9781487561161 (PDF) |
    ISBN 9781487561178 (EPUB)
Subjects: LCSH: Liberalism—Canada. | LCSH: Democracy—Canada. |
    LCSH: Liberty. | LCSH: Equality— Canada. | LCSH: Right and left
    (Political science)—Canada.
Classification: LCC JC574.2.C35 M33 2025 | DDC 320.510971—dc23

Cover design: Heng Wee Tan
Cover image: iStock.com/wisan224

We wish to acknowledge the land on which the University of Toronto Press
operates. This land is the traditional territory of the Wendat, the Anishnaabeg, the
Haudenosaunee, the Métis, and the Mississaugas of the Credit First Nation.

University of Toronto Press acknowledges the financial support of the Government
of Canada, the Canada Council for the Arts, and the Ontario Arts Council, an
agency of the Government of Ontario, for its publishing activities.

Canada Council   **Conseil des Arts**
for the Arts   **du Canada**

ONTARIO ARTS COUNCIL
CONSEIL DES ARTS DE L'ONTARIO

an Ontario government agency
un organisme du gouvernement de l'Ontario

Funded by the   Financé par le
Government   gouvernement
of Canada   du Canada

MIX
Paper | Supporting
responsible forestry
FSC   FSC® C016245
www.fsc.org

Contents

Foreword

When in mid-seventeenth century Thomas Hobbes described life as nasty, brutish, and short[1] he was not offering a morbid view of life on earth. Rather, he was speaking of human life in the absence of security, industry, culture, arts, letters, and society, and had in mind the human condition without the influences and processes of governance.[2] He likened it to a state of war of every person against every person,[3] a state – we might say – without politics.

Fast forward three centuries to Bernard Crick's *In Defence of Politics*.[4] Politics, Crick wrote, "is a way of ruling in divided societies without undue violence,"[5] and "most technologically advanced societies are divided societies, are pluralistic and not monolithic."[6] Political ethics, he said, "are not some inferior type of ethical activity, but are a level of ethical life fully self-contained and fully justifiable. Politics is not just a necessary evil; it is a realistic good."[7]

Politics so described is "a process of discussion,"[8] a dialectic or investigation of different and often conflicting possibilities, and is not peculiar to one theory or doctrine. "Politics is conservative – it preserves the minimum benefits of established order; politics is liberal – it is compounded of particular liberties and it requires tolerance; politics is socialist – it provides conditions for deliberate social change by which groups can come to feel that they have an equitable stake in the prosperity and survival of the community."[9]

The self-containment of politics as process must be defended against claims that would undermine it. The claims come from ideology: "ideological thinking is an explicit and direct challenge to political thinking;"[10] from democracy: while many claims of democracy are compatible with politics, there are some that can lead to despotism or anarchy[11]; from nationalism, which can lead people "to abandon or to scorn politics;"[12] and from technology which, when extended beyond scientific principles applied to the production of tools and goods, is "perverted into a social doctrine" which holds that "all the important problems facing human civilization are technical ... and soluble on the basis of existing knowledge or readily available knowledge – if sufficient resources are made available."[13]

There are other less intractable claims that must be resisted in the interest of politics. Within Crick's sights are those who claim to be above politics, or who wish to enjoy the fruits of politics without paying the price, or whose impatience "breeds a quest for certainty and a contempt for politics."[14] None of these "has a permanent tendency towards the real hatred of politics which characterizes ideological thought and totalitarian doctrines,"[15] but they must nonetheless be resisted.

It follows from Crick's analysis that politics rests on its own merits and the political virtues that make it possible – prudence, tolerance, compromise, and adaptability.[16] "It is an activity – lively, adaptive, flexible and conciliatory … and is the way in which free societies are governed."[17] Fast forward – again – over the decades since Crick wrote his classic, we must acknowledge that politics and its attendant virtues as he understood them are in decline. People are more polarized, ideologies more prominent, and ways of thinking and feeling have been conflated into ways of knowing, competing with science and reason. Illiberalism is threatening our politics, though it is not clear whether the threat is a passing phenomenon or a more lasting one. We need to find out.

Introduction

Illiberalism and liberalism compete for the attention of Canadians today. The latter honours values and features that we associate with Western democracies, particularly their democratic institutions and politics, established freedoms, equality of opportunity, and market economies. Illiberal voices challenging them have become more prominent in our politics, universities, and schools, and in public administration generally. They disparage historical understandings of Western democracy and seek to alter, fundamentally, its features and values. This book argues that the liberalism that has been a tenet of Canadian democracy for most of its history is in decline, resulting in diminished freedom of expression, a deteriorating political and policy environment, and fraying social cohesion.

Ours is not the first experience with an attack on liberalism. In the 1930s, fascist governments in Germany and

Italy, and Communists in the Soviet Union and elsewhere, saw Western liberal democracies as decadent and resorted to belligerence and aggression against them, triggering a world war. The difference today is that the illiberalism that threatens liberal democracies, including Canada, is found within them and takes aim at our politics, rights, and institutions from inside. It will not be rebuffed by military force, but it must be met by firm voices rejecting its excesses and affirming core values of liberalism and liberal democracy, and insisting upon their practice in our public life. Unless this happens, Canada will be in peril.

Our rights as individuals and our responsibilities as citizens of a democracy are essential topics in liberal discourse, and here we acknowledge an indebtedness to John Stuart Mill as a classical authority on the subject.[1] Mill asserted that society – individually or collectively – could legitimately interfere with the liberty of one of its members only in self-protection: "the only purpose for which power can be rightfully exercised over any member of a civilized community, against his will, is to prevent harm to others."[2] Mill recognized that members have social duties they may have to perform, including serving in common defence of the society that affords them protection.[3] He recognized, too, that "the fact of living in society renders it indispensable that each should be bound to observe a certain line of conduct towards the rest."[4] His was not a doctrine of "selfish indifference"[5] impervious to the social virtues that improve individual and collective well-being, but his focus was on freedom. He was insistent that human liberty requires freedom of conscience, thought, and feeling: "absolute freedom of opinion and sentiment on all subjects, practical or speculative, scientific, moral or theological."[6] And because freedom to express and publish "is practically inseparable"[7] from freedom of conscience and opinion, it too is included. Also included is a "liberty of tastes and pursuits, of framing the plan of our life to suit our own character, of doing what we like ... without impediment from our fellow citizens, so long as what we do does not harm them."[8] From this liberty it follows that individuals also have freedom of assembly "for any purpose not involving harm to others."[9]

There are differences of opinion on the legacy of Mill,[10] but his contribution to our understanding of liberalism remains relevant in the midst of contemporary reports that liberal democracy is faltering and perhaps failing. In the United States, Francis Fukuyama[11] argues that liberalism is in crisis and that in recent decades the principles of liberalism have "been pushed to new extremes by both the right and left: neo-liberals have made a cult of economic freedom and progressives have focused on identity over human universality as central to their political vision."[12] Mark Lilla[13] agrees that American liberalism is in crisis.[14] In recent decades, liberals have thrown themselves "into the movement politics of identity, losing a sense of what we share as citizens and what binds us as a nation."[15] Charles Noble[16] writes of the collapse of liberalism, arguing that it has been unable to solve problems of inequality. Though more pointedly stated in the United States, these arguments are heard in Canada too.

Our subject, then, is a broad one. It extends beyond our freedoms – political and economic – to our politics, the meaning of our citizenship, and to the institutions that must accommodate them and mediate their claims. My interest in the subject grew in the course of writing two of my previous books. In *University Commons Divided*[17] I wrote of growing differences within the academy between debate for which universities should be known and entrenched positioning in which debate is resisted and sometimes suppressed. In *Canada in Question*[18] I explored the contemporary meaning of our citizenship and some of the behaviours that undermine it. My perspectives find support in a 2022 study commissioned by the Macdonald-Laurier Institute. This study, by two professors,[19] finds that "there is a crisis in higher education in Canada."[20] A survey of professors and members of the public found that Canadian universities are "political monoliths" (overwhelmingly left-leaning) with serious consequences, including conservative professors who hide their political beliefs for fear of reprisals by colleagues, students, and others and who believe they face a hostile work environment; and widespread self-censorship practised by 57 per cent of right-leaning professors and 34 per cent of left-leaning professors who fear negative consequences from expressing their views. Most troubling is the finding that 30 per cent of professors are willing to limit academic freedom and "cancel" colleagues who do not share their political views on social justice issues.[21]

This study should be vigorously and openly debated. For my purposes, it raises a growing concern – and my hypothesis – that the principles and values of liberalism are under threat, not only in our universities but more widely in our public lives. Others before and with me share this concern. My contribution, I hope, shall be a systematic exploration of the threat from a Canadian perspective, with comparisons elsewhere, to determine its extent and magnitude, and to identify measures to counter it. Simply put, the question I ask is whether liberalism is being overtaken by illiberalism and with what consequences.

Chapter one will explore claims that are made in the name of freedom and in particular the growth of "freedom from" claims in addition to "freedom of" claims. Chapter two shall consider the decline of politics as understood by Crick. Chapter three will focus on hate in two dimensions: reckless attributions of hate directed by some people against those with whom they disagree, and the growing number of hate crimes in the Western world. Chapter four will study what is often seen as liberalism's greatest shortcoming: the persistence of inequality. Chapter five shall explore the calibre of institutions, leadership, and trust that are essential in a struggle against illiberalism. Chapter six will offer an overview with conclusions. An afterword shall conclude the volume.

I have acknowledgments, named and unnamed. I have relied on many thinkers, identified in the text and endnotes, with shared concerns about illiberalism. They have provided many of the building blocks on which I rest my analysis and conclusions. I believe that their numbers are growing, though they have not yet coalesced into the voices necessary for a concerted pushback and reversal of illiberal influences. Others to whom I am grateful include Michael Atkinson, a constant source of ideas, constructive criticism, and encouragement; and Pierre-Gerlier Forest with whom

I had helpful conversations about Crick's *Defence of Politics*. Others read parts of the manuscript or otherwise contributed to my thinking: Ken Coates, Margaret Kierylo, Siu Ming Kwok, Kevin McQuillan, Jack Mintz, Dwight Newman, and Lori Turnbull. I am thankful too for the support and encouragement of my family near and far, and for the work of Franquie Parkinson, my assistant during my assignment at the University of Calgary School of Public Policy, in preparing the manuscript for review. I add the necessary caveat that I alone am responsible for any shortcomings.

In 2012, University of Toronto President David Naylor introduced me to the University of Toronto Press, and this is my fourth book published with this excellent organization. I have been fortunate to have worked with editor Dan Quinlan on all four volumes, and I owe him more than I can say for the combination of guidance, advice, caution, and encouragement that he brings to his work. He played a major role in bringing this and previous books into print, and I thank him warmly.

I am indebted to others at the Press. The reports of two anonymous reviewers and the reader for the Manuscript Review Committee suggested revisions that improved the book. Ryan Pidhayny oversaw editorial stages in collaboration with Apex Project Management. Ashley Bernicky and Stephanie Mazza led in production and marketing. I thank them and the rest of the team at UTP.

CHAPTER 1

In Freedom's Name

In early 2022 what became known as the Freedom Convoy made its way across Canada to Ottawa. Hundreds of trucks and other vehicles, and thousands of truckers with other protesters, joined the convoy in what began as resistance to vaccine mandates and evolved as a wider movement in support of claiming or reclaiming freedom. The protesters and their trucks arrived in the city in late January and proceeded downtown where they parked on main streets and gridlocked the city centre, including Parliament Hill. They remained for three weeks, annoying and sometimes intimidating the city's downtown residents, with some behaving disrespectfully towards historical and other sites in the nation's capital. The prime minister invoked the country's Emergencies Act in mid-February, and police ended the blockade days later. The invocation of the Act was reviewed by Ontario Court of Appeal Justice Paul Rouleau, who in

February 2023 determined that it was justified but avoidable. Failures in policing, in federalism (failure to coordinate and cooperate across regions and governments), and in the Ontario government, he found, contributed to the national emergency that resulted in use of the legislation. He added a concession that is unusual in reports of this kind: "I do not come to this decision easily, as I do not consider the factual basis for it to be overwhelming. Reasonable and informed people could reach a different conclusion than the one I have arrived at."[1]

One person who reached a different conclusion is Federal Court Justice Richard Mosley, and his decision, unlike Justice Rouleau's opinion, has the force of law. In a ruling published in January 2024, he concluded that the decision to proclaim the Emergencies Act was unreasonable, unjustified, and contrary to the Charter of Rights and Freedoms: "The record does not support a conclusion that the Convoy had created a critical, urgent and temporary situation that was national in scope and could not effectively be dealt with under any other law of Canada."[2] The government has announced that it will appeal the decision, but it stands now as authority in support of a high threshold for the invocation of legislation that deprives Canadians of their rights.

At the beginning of the protest, truckers objected to vaccine mandates and quarantine measures for border crossings between Canada and the United States. Only a small minority of cross-border truckers were unvaccinated, though the numbers were large enough to raise supply chain issues. As the Convoy assembled and crossed the country, appeals to end all vaccine mandates and to a recovery of freedom were heard more frequently. At issue was not whether vaccinations against COVID were obligatory but whether restrictions faced by the unvaccinated were necessary to contain the virus and proportionate to its threats. In the case of the truckers these included quarantines on their return to the Canadian side of the border, which would curtail their ability to make a living from cross-border transport.

Charter rights are protected under the Emergencies Act, and it is clear that the truckers and other protesters had Charter freedoms of expression, peaceful assembly, and association subject to the section one stipulation of reasonable limits prescribed by law that can be demonstrably justified in a free and democratic society. These limits would reasonably include keeping the streets accessible to all users and curtailing mischief to public and private property. However, instead of clearing the streets or preventing the gridlock in the first place, and safeguarding national memorials like the tomb of the unknown soldier, officials, including the prime minister, vilified the protesters and froze the financial assets of hundreds of them. These fuelled a claim of freedom "from" an intrusive and aggressive government in addition to freedom "of" one or more enumerated rights.

Freedom "from" claims are becoming more common, and they are often associated with the political right. Leader of the opposition Pierre Poilievre has said that he wants to make Canada "the freest nation on earth,"[3] and his sentiments are echoed in the country's conservative circles. In that Canada already ranks near the top in political rights and civil liberties – sixth out of 152 countries, according to one source[4] – concern about our freedom must be about something else. For Poilievre, it is about gatekeepers[5] in or employed by government who stand between Canadians and their collective or individual goals. Reduce the size, intrusiveness, and inefficiencies of government, and Canadians will be freer to pursue those goals.

The left has its own freedom "from" claims arising in the context of identity politics. Alan Cairns distinguished between moderate and strong claims of this subject: the moderate version of identity politics "sensitizes society to expressions of difference that historically were suppressed, concealed or unvoiced"[6] and requires accommodation of them in public life. The strong version challenges representation and representative democracy: A cannot represent B because of their differences. "You have to be one to understand one or to represent one."[7] This version "encourages charges of 'voice appropriation' when 'outsiders' express opinions about experiences they have not had or identities they lack"[8] and can lead to a shunning of those outsiders. Trent University's Freedom Lounge is an illustration. This lounge is advertised to be for "students who identify as Indigenous, Black, Brown, Racialized and Students of Colour."[9] It proclaims intolerance for "homophobia, sexism, racism, anti-black racism, anti-Indigenous racism, Islamophobia, transphobia, xenophobia, ableism, classism or any other alternate forms of discrimination"[10] and prohibits debate of "Others' life experiences or the different experiences of oppression."[11] White students are excluded from those for whom the space was created; freedom "from" their voices is one of the objectives.

A similar example is found in the Black Student Space opened at the University of British Columbia in the fall of 2023. This is "an identity-affirming space available only for Black undergraduate and graduate students currently enrolled at UBC." White, Asian, or Indigenous complexions are unwelcome.

Universities in Canada and the United States have tolerated, if not embraced, the rise of identity politics, even its strong variant. In so doing they have aligned themselves *as institutions* with the pursuit of social justice and have become politicized. This is a departure from their core mission of seeking truth and the institutional neutrality necessary for its fulfilment, and threatens support for their cause among competing claims for tax and philanthropic dollars. Both UBC and Trent University are public institutions whose programs and facilities are supported by taxpayers of whatever origins or skin colours, and it should be axiomatic that discrimination against any in the university's public spaces is impermissible.[12]

There are other instances of freedom "from" claims. Blocking or silencing guest speakers whose views are deemed objectionable; demands for safe spaces free from unwelcome views; trigger warnings about course material that some may find disturbing; school boards burning books[13] or culling them because authors from years or centuries past are now seen as offensive; occasional shouting down of dissenting voices: these have all occurred and their impact is not only situational; they create a climate of repression, a silencing through a reluctance to speak out. It is difficult to measure the presence and extent of self-censorship, but it is reasonable to conclude that it is on the rise, and not only in Canada.

The United States has a long history of free speech issues on university and college campuses. In that country, as in Canada, it is important to know the impact of these issues on how participants and observers view their own and others' freedoms, and we have surveys to help inform us. The Knight Foundation, in cooperation with Gallup and Ipsos, has been measuring university and college student attitudes to free speech and the First Amendment[14] since 2016. Among key findings in 2022 is a reported steady decline in the number of students who think free speech rights are secure, with a 12 per cent decline since 2019. "More students now say the climate at school prevents some from saying things others might find offensive, and fewer feel comfortable disagreeing in class."[15] The Foundation for Individual Rights and Expression (FIRE) ranks campuses for these freedoms and found that 60 per cent of students "reported feeling that they could not express an opinion because of how students, a professor, or their administration would respond,"[16] and only 15 per cent reported "feeling very comfortable disagreeing with a professor about a controversial topic."[17] The concerns are not limited to students. A Gallup survey conducted for Inside Higher Ed in 2018 found that "only 41 percent of college and university leaders said that free speech rights are secure on the nation's campuses and only 36 percent said free speech is secure in the nation as a whole."[18]

In the United Kingdom, Academics for Academic Freedom have published a lengthy "Banned" List of individuals who have been prevented from speaking at UK universities or who have endured campaigns to silence or fire them.[19] In 2019, the government decided that intervention was necessary to establish protections for lawful free speech,[20] and in 2022 the Policy Institute at King's College London released a comprehensive report on student and public perceptions on free speech on campus.[21] According to the institute's policy director, Bobby Duffy, the study "reveals two main patterns – firstly, that the large majority of university students think their universities are protecting their freedom of speech, but secondly, that increasing minorities of students feel this is under threat and have heard of examples of free speech being inhibited."[22] Further, "[w]e can't divorce these trends in universities from changes in wider society, where we've seen increasing focus on 'culture war' issues which will influence student opinions."[23]

In Australia, former Chief Justice Robert French was appointed by the federal government to review free speech in the country's universities. In 2019, he reported that claims of a free speech crisis in Australian universities were not borne out, though he proposed that universities voluntarily adopt a code to protect academic freedom.[24] In New Zealand, the Free Speech Union graded the country's eight universities on academic freedom based on a survey of academics, written policies on the subject, and their records in allowing speakers on campus despite calls to ban them. One university achieved a failing grade; the others were assigned grades from C to A.[25]

Freedom of expression is foundational to liberalism, so reports that it is compromised are threatening. We noted in the introduction claims that liberalism is faltering, perhaps failing, and so we should turn to the thinking underlying these assessments. Columbia University's Mark Lilla, who is, in his words, a "frustrated American liberal,"[26] writes: "[m]y frustration has its source in an ideology that for decades has prevented liberals from developing an ambitious vision of America and its future that would inspire citizens of every walk of life and in every region of the country."[27] The ideology is identity politics. Instead of developing a new vision of America after the Reagan years, liberals "threw themselves into the movement politics of identity, losing a sense of what we share as citizens and what binds us as a nation."[28] Once about African Americans and women, identity politics, "by the 1980s … had given way to a pseudo-politics of self-regard and increasingly narrow and exclusionary self-definition that is now cultivated in our colleges and universities."[29]

> The focus of attention was now less on the relation between our identification with the United States as democratic citizens and our identification with different groups within it. Citizenship dropped out of the picture. And people began to speak instead of the inner homunculus, a unique little thing composed of parts tinted by race, sex and gender…. The only meaningful question became a deeply personal one: what does my country owe me by virtue of my identity?[30]

Answering this question may lead to conversation with others of like identity so that the question becomes, to paraphrase Lilla, what does our country owe us because of our shared identity?

Stanford University's Francis Fukuyama writes of two versions of identity politics. "One version sees the drive for identity as the completion of liberal politics: historically dominant elites fail to appreciate the specific struggles of marginalized groups, and therefore fail to recognize their underlying common humanity."[31] The second version "sees the lived experiences of different groups as fundamentally incommensurate; it denies the possibility of universally valid modes of cognition; and it elevates the value of group experience over what diverse individuals hold in common."[32] Fukuyama worries that in our time "the principles of liberalism have ... been pushed to new extremes by both the right and the left: neo-liberals have made a cult of economic freedom, and progressives have focused on identity over human universality as central to their political vision."[33]

Charles Noble of the State University of California argues that "the political assertion of identities, particularly national and ethnic identities, too readily devolves into a narrow, insular politics."[34] Even mild versions of identity politics "can prove problematic for the left because it makes it difficult to forge broad coalitions around shared interests. Rather than asserting common ties and identifying shared demands that might provide the basis for large, governing coalitions, political movements that stress their own, particular histories of oppression and self-affirmation can too easily become isolated one from another."[35]

Lilla and Fukuyama look to the reform of liberalism; Noble writes of its collapse and asserts a need for a new left. We shall later consider the futures they have in mind, but we should return now to our Canadian setting. Historically, both Liberal and Progressive Conservative parties could lay claim to supporting liberalism with a small l, but both parties have shifted ground on the political spectrum. Shedding the progressive label, and with its present leadership in Ottawa and some provinces, the Conservative Party has moved significantly to the right. But the Liberal Party too has changed. Jeffrey Simpson explains what he calls the decoupling of the party from its historical moorings: it once "anchored its appeal in a strong sense of Canadian pride, spending where appropriate but not excessively, defending Ottawa against provincial demands for more autonomy, and reflecting the country's linguistic duality."[36]

These moorings are now

> rusted or gone. The government's feminist orientation has attracted support among women, but this orientation is only one part "of a 'progressive' thinking in which politics ... goes beyond gender to appeals based on the identity of race, Indigeneity and sexual orientation. The Liberals under Justin Trudeau have been in the vanguard of this narrative, reflecting and abetting trends in the English-Canadian intelligentsia, cultural and educational institutions, museums and galleries, publishing houses and the Canadian Broadcasting Corporation.[37]

Abandoning unity and patriotism, "Mr. Trudeau has apologized more often than any prime minister for more past wrongs while almost never speaking about past accomplishments."[38]

> Under today's Liberals, and for most of the English-Canadian
> cultural class and institutions, Canada's past is a sad litany
> of sins unleavened by triumphs of the human spirit or gen-
> erosity. Polls – for example, those taken by Angus Reid –
> show that pride of country has declined among those under
> 30 years of age, although it remains high among the gar-
> den-variety Canadians who do not see that pride in Justin
> Trudeau's Liberal Party. The majority of those Canadians
> are prepared to acknowledge and atone for past sins such as
> residential schools, but they are not prepared to have their
> country defined by their prime minister and his party as an
> unbridled legacy of wrongdoing, genocide and racism.[39]

Simpson believes that Canadian politics may now be seen
to be about "polarizing voters around identity and ideology,"[40] and if so, the country is "more polarized than it has
ever been."[41]

Liberalism in the small l sense may be at risk, though
reports of its collapse are premature and we should consider its requirements for survival. This task shall be with
us throughout this book, and we begin here by identifying
essential features of liberalism in 2022. Four propositions are
germane: 1) Freedom of expression remains foundational to
liberalism; 2) it is freedom of expression that is to be protected,
not immunity for some from the expression of others; 3) only
the moderate view of identity politics (as described by Alan
Cairns and Francis Fukuyama) is compatible with liberalism;

and 4) our universities and colleges must protect freedom of expression and act against those who would undermine it. We shall now consider these propositions in order.

Freedom of expression is described by former Chief Justice Beverley McLachlin as "the indispensable condition of nearly every other freedom."[42] "Not only is the guarantee of central concern to free and democratic societies, it potentially is broad enough to cover all variety of activities. If the guarantee traditionally has been linked to political freedom, freedom of expression has expanded well beyond its roots in democracy to encompass nearly all non-violent forms of expression."[43] This freedom must have legal support, of course, but it must have rhetorical support too, and we must give voice to its centrality in liberal democracy and resist claims that would compromise it.

Freedom of expression is to be distinguished from claims to be free from the words and lawful actions of others. We see these claims in Trent University's Freedom Lounge where the voices of white students are not invited, and more generally in silencing those whose views are deemed objectionable; demands to be free from perspectives thought to be unsafe or offensive; burning or suppressing books and shouting down those with whom there is disagreement. Of course, there are legal limits to freedom of expression – defamation and prohibitions of hate speech, for example – and its unwise or intolerant exercise may incur social or professional disapprobation, but this freedom must, subject to law, have unqualified protection.

We come again to identity politics while noting the moderate and strong variants of the subject voiced by Canada's

Cairns and America's Fukuyama. Humans have multiple identities, with different ones finding expression depending upon time and circumstances. This is not only unobjectionable; it is inevitable, and a population may be called upon to compensate for identities of citizens that have been overlooked in public life. However, the strong version of identity politics divides the population into factions with little inclination to collaborate with one another. The situation is aggravated by social media, which creates virtual walls behind which the like-minded communicate and commiserate, sometimes adopting aggressive and uncompromising postures towards outsiders. Our conclusion follows: the moderate variant of identity politics is compatible with liberalism; the strong version is an affront to it.

This chapter concludes on the subject of universities and colleges. It is within these institutions that we should expect to find the strongest protections for freedom of expression. In my 2018 book *University Commons Divided*, I considered examples that tested freedom of expression on campus. I concluded that our universities and colleges were falling short of their responsibilities, and the question follows: have intervening years seen any change in this area?

Perhaps the best-known case in intervening years is that of Lyndsey Shepherd. She was a graduate student and teaching assistant at Wilfred Laurier University who showed her communications class clips of debates with psychologist Jordan Peterson on adding gender identity or expression as a prohibited ground of discrimination under the Canadian Human Rights Act and the Criminal Code. She took a neutral stance in the debates, but one of her students expressed concern about the clips to an LGBTQ support group, which resulted in a meeting with the university's manager of gender violence prevention, her supervisor, and the head of her academic program. We know precisely what happened at the meeting because, on the advice of her mother, Shepherd recorded the proceedings.

Shepherd was not shown a complaint and was not given a name. She was accused of creating a toxic climate for some of the students by playing the clips while maintaining a neutral stance. Her professor told her that the pronoun debate was comparable to discussing whether students of colour should have rights and said that playing the Peterson clip was like neutrally playing a speech by Hitler. The professor and manager of gender violence added that Peterson's position was unlawful. After Shepherd released the recording to the media, her supervisor and the university president apologized and a lawyer who was asked to conduct an independent investigation exonerated Shepherd from any wrongdoing.

The episode is ongoing through a defamation lawsuit launched by Peterson, and there is irony in the university resting its defence in part on the claim that what its officials said about him was an exercise of their free expression.[44] Their comparison of Peterson to Hitler was egregious and defamatory on its face, but the case will likely turn on whether there was publication as required by the law of defamation and, if so, whether the university bears the responsibility for publishing the defamatory statements. Whatever the outcome, the episode was a clear case of overreach and unprofessionalism on the part of the professors and administrator who met with Shepherd. It is worth repeating that the impact of her case and other examples is not only situational. They contribute to a chilling effect on freedom of expression and, in the Shepherd case, academic freedom. Progressives are less worried about this than persons of conservative disposition, probably because it is their narrative that is dominant in our universities and other public institutions. But political differences should not matter where freedoms are at stake. Freedom of expression is only as strong for all of us as it is for less popular or minority views.

Conclusion

John Stuart Mill's harm principle allowed that our freedoms are limited only by the stipulation that their exercise must not harm others. The potential reach of that stipulation is expanded by claims that we must be free from words and behaviours that are lawful though perceived as offensive by those who hear or witness them. The wider the stipulation's coverage, the narrower the freedom.

Vaccine mandates are not an affront to liberalism. Some may choose to be unvaccinated and to defend that choice as a personal and private one, and it is, provided that it is made by a competent person and the targeted affliction is not contagious. If, however, the affliction is contagious, a decision to refuse vaccination is not a personal one because the contagion threatens harm, perhaps death, to others. Vaccine mandates were necessary to deal with COVID; whether the mandates were reasonable and proportionate to the threat is an issue of public policy to be debated and determined accordingly.

Claims to freedom from the lawful behaviour of unwelcome persons and voices must also fail. We may complain about speakers whose views we don't like; books we find offensive, or people we don't want around us, and in our private lives we are free to govern ourselves accordingly by skipping the speech, avoiding the books, and socializing only with those we want nearby. But our public lives intersect with others, and we do not have rights to be free from their presence in the public commons or from their lawful words and conduct. Tolerance for the rights and freedoms of others is foundational to liberalism.

CHAPTER 2

The Decline of Politics

We recall Bernard Crick's description of politics as "an activity – lively, adaptive, flexible and conciliatory," and we recall too the virtues that make it work – prudence, tolerance, compromise, and adaptability.[1] Its practice throughout our modern history has been notable, at no time more than in the years following the Second World War. The establishment of the United Nations in 1945 and of NATO in 1949, and the early origins of the European Union were landmark political developments aimed at preventing a recurrence of that war's legacy, and ushered in a liberal, rules-based order that prevailed in the West for the decades that followed. America's Anne Applebaum observes that this "liberal world order relied on the mantra of 'Never again.' Never again would there be genocide. Never again would larger nations erase smaller nations from the map. Never again would we be taken in by dictators who used the language of mass murder."[2]

In 2016, Canada's Colin Robertson observed that "the liberal international order … is under severe strain."[3] Two years later, former Governor-General David Johnston wrote of "the collapse of the liberal democratic consensus that stayed largely intact for some five decades following the end of the Second World War."[4] Applebaum, too, concluded that the liberal world order had ended: "[t]here is no natural liberal world order, and there are no rules without someone to enforce them."[5] But she is not without hope: "maybe there is no natural liberal world order, but there are liberal societies, open and free countries that offer a better chance for people to live useful lives than closed dictatorships do."[6] There follows her admonishment: "[p]recisely because there is no liberal world order, no norms and no rules, we must fight ferociously for the values and hopes of liberalism if we want our open societies to continue to exist."[7]

What does a ferocious fight for liberalism entail? We saw in chapter one that supporting freedom of expression limited only by law is part of the fight. Defending politics as conceived by Crick from those who would undermine or diminish it is another part. He saw ideology as a principal foe of politics, particularly when combined with totalitarianism. The "sharpest contrast"[8] with political rule is totalitarianism: "[t]he totalitarian believes that everything is relevant to government and that the task of government is to reconstruct society utterly according to the goals of an ideology."[9] Crick had in mind the twentieth-century experience with communism and fascism in which the defence of politics failed and ideologues ruled in totalitarian settings.

For the defence to succeed, ideologies must be identified and contained – by politics, of course.

Is ideology – "a system of ideas that aspires both to explain the world and to change it"[10] – a present threat to liberalism? We do not see signs of a dramatic, seismic shift in liberal democracies, nor do we see the emergence of mass movements that Hannah Arendt reminds us are precursors to seismic shifts of this kind.[11] The current play of ideology is more limited, but over time it may be just as threatening. In Canada we see it in a growing schism between those who identify either as progressives or conservatives, resulting in a more polarized politics. In the United States, the polarization between Democrats and Republicans is intense, and there is real or threatened violence by mini-militias linked to extremist groups and even their prospective victims.[12] The threats from these developments should not be underestimated. Harvard University's Steven Levitsky and Daniel Ziblatt tell us that America's democratic norms are being weakened by extreme partisan polarization. "And if one thing is clear from studying breakdowns throughout history, it's that extreme polarization can kill democracies."[13]

A related threat is populism. The word is not used with precision,[14] and the wide eligibility for its use is explained by Cas Mudde and Cristobal Rovira in their description of populism as a "thin-centered ideology"[15]: "expressions of populism are almost always combined with very different (thin and full) ideologies such as conservatism, liberalism, nativism or 'Americanismo.' This implies that in the real world there are few, if any, pure forms of populism (in isolation) but, rather, subtypes of it, which show a specific articulation of certain ideological features."[16]

There is agreement, however, that populism "is predicated upon the positing of an antagonistic relationship between two collective identities: 'the people' and 'the elites.'"[17] Harvard University's Norm Gidron and Bart Bonikowski "focus on three main conceptual approaches that emerge out of the political science and sociology literature on the topic"; they define populism, respectively, as "an ideology, a discursive style, and a form of political mobilization."[18] With respect to the first, populism "is first and foremost a set of ideas caused by an antagonism between the people and the elite, as well as the primacy of popular sovereignty, whereby the virtuous general will is placed in opposition to the moral corruption of elite actors."[19] With the second, populism as discursive style, we hear the rhetoric of "us versus them" from left, right, or in between, depending on context. The third, populism as political strategy, "comprises three variants that focus on different aspects of the subject: policy choices, political organization, and forms of mobilization."[20]

We should note as one of its features that populism "is typically critical of representation and anything that mediates the relation between the people and their leader or government."[21] In a contest between people and elites, the people will count representatives, officials, and bureaucrats among the elites and, therefore, among their political foes. This has two consequences: first, it tends to sideline the institutions of governance in which representatives, officials, and bureaucrats are engaged, and second, it attributes an elevated status to the leader, who pays scant attention to legal, constitutional, or administrative constraints on his power. Implementing populist will is what matters, not adhering to the protocols of democracy.

Gidron and Bonikowski's second conceptual approach – populism as discursive style – is developed by Elena Block and Ralph Negrine, who offer "a critical framework that integrates three key categories to identify and analyze the most relevant features of the populist communication style: identity, rhetoric and use of the media."[22] Identity is key to the role played by populist leaders in the construction of "the people," a notion that loosely brings together all those with "unfulfilled demands, a group destined to break the status quo, take power from the ruling elite (the Other) and build a new ... populist order."[23] Their rhetoric "involves adversarial, emotional, patriotic and abrasive speech through which they connect with the discontented. They use multiple channels of political communication to transmit their messages and connect with their publics."[24]

The third conceptual approach outlined by Gidron and Bonikowski – political strategy – is the operational one, and here we note the argument of Michael Hetherall that when populists acquire executive power, "they will be driven to align their strategic choices to their populist narrative."[25]

It is no surprise ... that President Trump's most important foreign policy decisions and statements have directly aligned with his campaign narrative of U.S. leaders making bad deals with foreign countries. The decision to pull out of multilateral agreements such as the Trans-Pacific Partnership and the Paris Agreement, the imposition of trade tariffs and efforts to unsettle the existing trade relationship with China, belligerent language towards traditional allies and constant criticism of domestic elites who allowed supposed bad deals to occur, all represent an alignment of a populist narrative with grand strategy.[26]

The University of Amsterdam's Claes H. de Vreese and his colleagues point to positive features of populism:

> Populism might increase representation and give a voice to groups of citizens that do not feel heard by the current political elite. Populism might broaden the attention for issues that are not in the mainstream news. Populism might mobilize groups of people that have felt on the fringe of the political system. Populism might improve the responsiveness of the political system by making actors and parties align their policies more with the "wishes of the people." Populism might be a refreshing wake-up call to power-holders, prompting periodic reflections on their conduct and elitism.[27]

But populism also "constitutes a fundamental challenge to the institutions and values of liberal democracy."[28] It may "curb minority rights" or "use the electoral mandate to erode independent institutions that are considered cornerstones of existing democracies, like the courts or the free media."[29] It may "lead to political tribalism, which impedes civil discourse and discourages political compromise."[30] Populism rejects pluralism – an understanding that "values are often in conflict" and that "demands of justice, fairness, freedom and equality ... often point in different directions.

There's no universally accepted ordering of such values so good people will disagree on what's right. The purpose of liberal democracy is to accommodate these disagreements and let people live together peaceably despite them."[31]

The practice of populism further undermines liberal democracy. Moises Naim observes that "despite differences in culture, history, political systems, or the economic circumstances of the countries where populism is now being deployed, populist leaders resort to the same tactics: they practice divide and conquer; they magnify their country's problems and criminalize the opposition; they play up external threats while claiming that foreign enemies are in the midst of those at home; they glorify the military, discredit experts, and attack the media."[32]

The contrast between the practice and values of politics as conceived by Crick – and populism – is stark. We turn first to the United States and to what can fairly be described as a populist uprising. On 6 January 2021, as the Trump administration was in its final days, thousands of the president's supporters gathered in Washington, DC, as Congress prepared to confirm Biden's election win. Incited by the outgoing president, the gathering turned into a mob bent on infiltrating, mocking, and disrupting the institutions and processes of American democracy. The immediate consequences were serious: casualties among the mob and those deployed to resist it and appeals for Trump's ouster two weeks before the inauguration of his successor. The longer-term consequences are serious too.

One year after the uprising, one observer wrote that "Donald Trump and his allies continue to promote the 'Big

Lie' that the election was stolen from them,"[33] an accusation echoed in other Republican election losses, including the 2022 Arizona governor's race in which the Trump-endorsed candidate sought a court order to overturn her election loss by 17,000 votes.[34] The most startling consequence was Trump's call in December 2022 to set aside the US Constitution. He wrote: "Do you throw the Presidential Election Results of 2020 OUT and declare the RIGHTFUL WINNER, or do you have a NEW ELECTION? Massive fraud of this type and magnitude allows for the termination of all rules, regulations and articles, even those found in the Constitution."[35] Troubling as it is that this appeal is made by a former president of the United States, it is more troubling that his claims continue to be supported by millions of Americans. Most Republican voters continue to believe the 2020 election was stolen from Trump, with 21 million who believe that the use of violence to restore his presidency is justified.[36] Perhaps some of their minds will be changed by the release, in December 2022, of the House January 6 committee report.[37] The committee of seven Democrats and two Republicans was unanimous in finding that Trump conspired to defeat the will of voters and recommended criminal charges against the former president, including conspiracy to defraud the United States, obstruction of the certification of Biden's election win, conspiracy to make a false statement, and inciting insurrection.

The repercussions from the assault on Congress will not end with the January 6 committee report. Trump remains unrepentant: "these folks don't get it that when they come after me, people who love freedom rally around me. It strengthens me. What doesn't kill me makes me stronger."[38] He is seeking a return to the White House, though his May 2024 felony convictions could prevent him from realizing this ambition.

His response was to label the special counsel in the case against him a "deranged psycho,"[39] and his supporters remain staunch in his defence.

Whatever may be the political fate of Trump, his re-election bid prompted one observer to write that "[t]he populist revolt is bigger than Trump and it always has been."[40] This is true in the United States and on an international scale: according to one report[41] there have been forty-six populist leaders or political parties that have led thirty-three countries between 1990 and 2018 – a fivefold increase in numbers over those same years, and it appears that the momentum has not abated since 2018.[42]

Until recently, Canadians were complacent about populism because it has not flourished here despite populist influences in our history.[43] But the freedom convoy has shaken our complacency. It is seen by some as a populist protest, though its origins belie that description; it was a mass demonstration, with different motivations drawing participants and sympathizers together. However, as Dale Eisler and Kevin Lynch observe, it illustrates a more severe divide among Canadians: "In recent years, Canada has become a cauldron of ever more heated political rhetoric and emotions, often drawn on regional, rural-urban and identity lines. Importing some of the worst aspects of today's American politics, social media platforms have enabled misinformation, conspiracy theories, identity politics and wedge issues to fester and divide in Canada."[44] Neither of the two main parties – Liberals or Conservatives – have worked to bridge differences with the result that "the centre of Canadian politics is being hollowed out."[45]

There are populist influences in some of our political parties – Maxime Bernier's People's Party on the federal level and Premier Danielle Smith's United Conservative Party in Alberta are examples, though neither exhibits the stridency we have seen in the United States and elsewhere. In addition, we should be cautious about concluding that growing polarization will be permanent or long-standing. There have been enduring features of the moderate left and right in Canadian politics that may resurface in time. Federal Liberals believe in the power of government to do what they see as good things, and there is no end to their list of good things to do. Federal Conservatives envision a more limited role for government, focusing on matters within federal jurisdiction and conceding wider latitude to the provinces and to individual responsibility. Rather than a steady and irreversible drift to a more divided polity, tensions and divisions may wax and wane depending upon the leadership and politics of the day.

Populism is aggravated by a decline in Enlightenment values. Harvard University's Canadian American psychologist Steven Pinker writes about the legacy of the Enlightenment and its underlying themes – reason, science, humanism, and progress[46] – that dominated European ideas from the 1700s to the 1900s:

If there's anything the Enlightenment thinkers had in common, it was an insistence that we energetically apply the

standard of reason to understanding our world, and not
fall back on generators of delusion like faith, dogma, rev-
elation, authority, charisma, mysticism, divination, visions,
gut feelings, or the hermeneutic parsing of sacred texts....
The deliberate application of reason was necessary precisely
because our common habits of thought are not particularly
reasonable.[47]

Steven Pinker believes that Enlightenment themes – and
values – continue to be confronted by human inclinations for
"loyalty to tribe, deference to authority, magical thinking,
the blaming of misfortune on evildoers"[48] and that they "are
treated by today's intellectuals with indifference, skepticism
and sometimes contempt."[49] He rejects the language of right
and left, and the ideologies along the spectrum, in favour
of treating societies "as ongoing experiments"[50] allowing us
to learn best practices regardless of whether they are left,
right, or in between. "The empirical picture at present suggests that people flourish most in liberal democracies with a
mixture of civic norms, guaranteed rights, market freedom,
social spending and judicious regulation."[51] But this picture
is at odds with ideologues and with "religious, political
and cultural pessimists who insist that Western civilization
is in terminal decline."[52] Pinker argues that the evidence
supports the opposite conclusion. "The Enlightenment has
worked – perhaps the greatest story seldom told,"[53] and he
is not alone in celebrating the Enlightenment. Before him,
Albert Salomon wrote that the "desire for enlightened vigi-
lance and praise of the Enlightenment are appropriate in
the contemporary age of irrational modes of thinking and

acting."[54] More recently, Anthony Pagden has shown "how Enlightenment concepts directly influence modern culture, making possible a secular, tolerant and, above all, cosmopolitan world,"[55] and Tzvetan Todorov has praised the Enlightenment's "celebration of plurality, of difference, of the idea that debate is healthy and productive."[56]

Critics of the Enlightenment "and its ideological child, liberalism,"[57] are found on the left and right. From the left, according to Stephen Bonner, Enlightenment values have "come under assault" from "anarchists, communitarians, post-modernists, half-hearted liberals and authoritarian socialists"[58]:

> Ideals long associated with reactionary movements – the privileging of experience over reasoning, national or ethnic identity over internationalism and cosmopolitanism, the community over the individual, custom over innovation, myth over science – have entered the thinking of the American left.... The collapse of intellectual coherence on the left reflects the collapse of a purposeful politics from the left.[59]

From the right, again according to Bonner, "anti-Enlightenment and anti-modern prejudices" persist as conservative thinkers "obsess about sexual license and the decline of family values, cultural 'nihilism' and the loss of tradition, tolerance for divergent life-styles and the erosion of national identity."[60]

Either populism or weakened Enlightenment values undermines liberal democracy, and the two in tandem increase the threat because each magnifies the other: populism accelerates a decline in Enlightenment values and is, in turn, strengthened by a flight from reason, science, and humanism. They make more complex and pluralistic societies more susceptible to factions arrayed against one another and rulers they perceive as controlling their lives. Fragmentation into groups of like-minded individuals, strategizing with one another on social media, and turning away from those with whom they disagree, diminishes the wide, continuing, and often difficult conversations necessary for democratic life.

While populist voices in Canada have so far been contained, their volume is increasing, and the threat to Enlightenment values is as discernible in this country as it is elsewhere. Especially troubling is the threat to them in our universities where some students and faculty treat those who disagree with them as not simply in error but in sin: "I am right, you are wrong and therefore a wrongdoer." They are not above threats, nor are they above shouting down those with whom they disagree in efforts to silence them and to embed their own views on social justice in university policy. Doubters on this count might turn again to the 2022 Macdonald-Laurier Institute study, previously referenced,[61] with its reports of extensive professorial, fearful self-censorship, and the willingness of nearly one-third of professors surveyed to limit academic freedom and "cancel" colleagues with whom they disagree on issues of social justice. If Enlightenment values are not as protected as they should be in our universities, we cannot expect them to flourish more widely.

Conclusion

We should not idealize Crick's view of politics. It is a competitive activity that attracts its share of egotists, self-promoters,
and individuals whose ambitions outweigh their contribu-
tions. But it also attracts people who are drawn to public life
to offer their services to improve the lot of their fellow citizens. Politics gives voters the opportunity to assess people
and programs and to choose freely from among them, and
it requires their choices to work across differences to govern
peacefully.

Politics with the attributes described by Crick has been
diminished in Canada. It may be "lively," but the adjectives
"adaptive," "flexible," and "conciliatory" are less applicable,
and the virtues that make it possible – prudence, compromise, tolerance, and adaptability – are not on ready display.
Censorious actors, some in our universities, are intolerant
of views that differ from theirs and are willing to suppress
them. Aggressive and judgmental voices more prone to
condemnation than to debate are heard more widely, resulting in a more stifling culture in which many people choose
to remain silent rather than endure abuse. And, as Jeffrey
Simpson,[62] Dale Eisler, and Kevin Lynch[63] point out, our
country has become more divided than at any time in our
recent history.

Weaker freedom of expression, ideology, populism, and a
decline in Enlightenment values, cumulatively, may prove
lethal to the politics of a huge, pluralistic, and decentralized
federation. We should recall Levitsky and Ziblatt's warning

that democracy "no longer ends with a bang – in a revolution or military coup – but with a whimper: the slow, steady weakening of critical institutions, such as the judiciary and the press, and the gradual erosion of long-standing political norms."[64] We should take heed before the decline of our politics becomes irreversible.

CHAPTER 3

Confronting Hate

The 1966 Report of the Special Committee on Hate Propaganda in Canada – a committee that included a future prime minister, a future minister of justice, and a sitting law dean – proposed that the incitement or promotion of hatred be made offences under the Criminal Code.[1] It was, at the time, a controversial initiative because of concern that it might undermine freedom of expression, "a main cornerstone of our way of life."[2] Already there were crimes and civil wrongs that could potentially address the promotion of hatred, and a hateful motive could be an aggravating factor in sentencing for many offences,[3] but these did not curb the nefarious behaviours. The new crimes were added in 1970: the advocacy or promotion of genocide defined as killing members of an identifiable group or deliberately inflicting on an identifiable group conditions of life calculated to bring about the group's physical destruction; communicating statements in a public place that incite hatred against any identifiable group where such incitement is likely to lead to a breach of the peace; and the communication, except in private conversation, of statements that wilfully promote hatred against an identifiable group.[4] Hatred is not statutorily defined but in *R. v. Keegstra*[5] the Supreme Court of Canada said that it connoted "emotion of an intense and extreme nature that is clearly associated with vilification and detestation." Further,

> Hatred is predicated on destruction, and hatred against identifiable groups therefore thrives on insensitivity, bigotry and destruction of both the target group and of the values of our society. Hatred in this sense is a most extreme emotion that belies reason; an emotion that, if exercised against members of an identifiable group, implies that those individuals are to be despised, scorned, denied respect and made subject to ill-treatment on the basis of group affiliation.[6]

The burden of proving hatred to this extent, the requirement of communication in public, and the stipulation that the hate be directed at an identifiable group meant that there would be few prosecutions under the legislation, and this has been the experience. Behaviours falling short of promoting or inciting hatred, but which are motivated by it, may constitute other crimes, most notably assaults, and there have been sharp increases of them in recent years.[7]

We might wonder what members of the Special Committee would say in 2023. They were particularly sensitive about freedom of expression, arguing that "the case for restraint must be shown to be very strong indeed."[8] From this starting point they would need to address two large, contemporary issues – the growth of hate crimes and the shrinking domain of free expression. With respect to the latter, allegations of hate intended to silence its sources are more common today, as are phobias attributed by some groups to those they perceive as foes, for example, Islamophobes or transphobes. In addition, there are examples of encroachment on freedom of expression that would have been unheard of decades ago: an experienced and highly qualified teacher who was suspended and subsequently fired by the Abbotsford School District after he observed, in class discussion, that most of the deaths of children in residential schools resulted from disease, mainly tuberculosis[9]; a member of Parliament who sought legislation that would make it a hate crime to take issue with the description of residential school history as genocide[10]; and "a toxic, in-your face activism"[11] that was practised by trans community demonstrators during a 2019 public address by a writer at the Toronto Public Library. Reviews of the daily news reveal that these are not isolated examples. A Barrie, Ontario, teacher found her job in peril after taking issue with critical race theory on a private Facebook page for teachers.[12] She wrote: "Kids aren't in school to be indoctrinated with critical race theory. Schools should be non-partisan. Focus on modeling kindness to everyone and speak out against any form of discrimination you see." This earned her a suspension without pay in 2021, a suspension she is still fighting. She observes, "There's an illiberal ideology that has been gaining traction for the last couple of decades and sped up in the last few years. The only acceptable philosophy nowadays among teachers is that teaching is a political act and that inculcating children with social justice values that stem from this illiberal ideology is not only justified but it's necessary."[13]

The "vogue for public shaming and ostracism"[14] that is now part of our culture is the subject of an open letter signed by 150 writers, including Margaret Atwood, Noam Chomsky, Malcolm Gladwell, JK Rowling, Salman Rushdie, and Gloria Steinem. They and others write: "The free exchange of information and ideas, the lifeblood of a liberal society, is daily becoming more constricted."[15] As writers, they say, "we need a culture that leaves us room for experimentation, risk-taking and even mistakes. We need to preserve the possibility of good-faith disagreement without dire professional consequences."[16]

We might add that disagreement about the full impact of residential schools, or whether Canada committed genocide, does not make dissenters anti-Indigenous. Differences on the relationship between a person's gender identity and biological sex does not make people anti-trans. Differences about critical race theory do not make critics racist. Failure to recognize these differences contributes to diminished free expression and the culture described in the open letter. It is a culture of denunciation and silencing in which people are reluctant to speak out against behaviours at odds with liberalism. We saw this in the Macdonald-Laurier Institute study of self-censorship in our universities. We see it to an equal or greater extent on campuses in the United States.[17]

The second large issue is the growth of real hate crimes. Their growth during the pandemic is a reminder that in times of stress and instability, there is a human tendency to look for someone to blame, a tendency that often settles on the "other" who is different in race, colour, religion, or other respects. When this tendency is intense and extreme, it features hate at the level described by the Supreme Court in *R. v. Keegstra* and is manifested in threatening or violent behaviour towards the "other." Numbers are increasing, and not only in Canada. In the United States, hate crimes increased by 12 per cent in 2021 over 2020.[18] In Great Britain, there has been a steady increase in hate crimes over the past decade and an increase in 2021/22 of about 25 per cent over 2020/21.[19] In its most recent report, "the Council of Europe warns that Europe is facing a shocking reality: antisemitic, anti-Muslim and other racist hate crimes are increasing at an alarming rate."[20] Examples tell us that the problem is not limited to Western countries: inter-tribal hate and violence persist in Africa, Rwanda and Kenya being recent examples.[21] In China's Xinjiang province, persecution of the Uyghur population has intensified. In Afghanistan, the return to power of the Taliban renews the threat against the Hazara people, said by some to be the "most persecuted people in the world."[22]

The struggle against illiberalism must include confronting hate. Crime motivated by hate is an affront to the entire country, and we must ask if we are doing all we reasonably can to reverse the increase and reduce the incidence. An uncomfortable question is whether the emphasis on our differences that is so common in the public commons today contributes more to a divide than to a cohesive whole. "Diversity is our strength," proclaims the prime minister, and it is a strength if meant in an evolution to a more cosmopolitan country and world. But in this era of identity politics, it may also reinforce a more parochial tendency – a hunkering down in social media and elsewhere with others of like identity and a turning away from those who are different, the other or others. Turning away from the other may breed belligerence and sometimes violence, perhaps even hate crimes.

Of course, we cannot definitively answer our uncomfortable question, but it does tell us that we need to understand the origins of hateful behaviours, among them prejudices from early childhood nurtured by family or associates who share them; and susceptibility to purveyors of hate online and elsewhere. Where these are not addressed by education, social disapproval, and regulating online platforms, we must turn again to the blunt instrument of the criminal law. Denunciation, restraint, and prevention are the goals here, and we turn to the question Shakespeare asked through Juliet: "What's in a name?"[23] The criminal law attaches labels to behaviours, and the names are important. Murder is the most serious homicide; robbery is a theft with real or threatened violence; kidnapping, embezzlement, fraud. Rape would have been on the list until 1982 when it became sexual assault, a name change prompted by considerations that included perceived stigmatization of victims. The names convey a sense of the criminal behaviours they describe and the seriousness with which they are viewed. In comparison, assault is a generic name that may apply to a range of behaviours, from the relatively harmless to the very serious. Assaults motivated by hatred of an identifiable group are among the very serious and should be singled out by naming the offence and identifying severe consequences that follow. They should be included as aggravated assaults in our criminal code, for example, everyone commits an aggravated assault, punishable on indictment by imprisonment for up to fourteen years, who commits an assault motivated by hatred of the complainant's membership in a group identified by race, colour, gender, religion, or sexual orientation.

Similarly, mischief is a generic term and crime that may include a wide range of behaviours, from minor acts of vandalism to serious and threatening obstruction, defacement, or destruction of property. A current example was the 10 November 2023 action of a group dubbed the Indigo 11 targeting Jewish businesswoman Heather Reisman and her downtown Toronto Indigo bookstore by smearing the window over her likeness with red paint and labelling her a funder of genocide. That the incident occurred on the anniversary of Kristallnacht – the 1938 Nazi-inspired attack on Jewish property in Germany – is presumably coincidence but is a reminder that conduct of this kind in a context that has seen a rise in anti-Semitism has the potential to escalate into acts of violence directed against Jewish people. The criminal charges against the Indigo 11 include mischief, and we do not yet know whether some or any of them were motivated by hate, but if so, the crime and criminal record should disclose the fact. Like assault, mischief is a hybrid offence – punishable on indictment or summary conviction – with severity determined by whether the damage exceeds $5,000. Mischief motivated by hate, like assault motivated by hate, should be a distinct offence punishable on indictment by serious criminal penalties.

Conclusion

Care must be taken in the attribution of hate; there are individuals and groups who view those who disagree with them as hateful, and they should be held accountable in the court of public opinion for their loose and reckless accusations of hate. But real hate (that meets the *Keegstra* definition) and hate crimes are on the increase and must be confronted. The Special Committee on Hate Propaganda did part of the job but left unaddressed hate crimes that do not amount to genocide, incitement, or promotion of hatred. The resulting gap should be addressed by designating assaults and mischief motivated by hate as separate aggravated crimes under the Criminal Code. These offences should be vigorously prosecuted with the motive part of the offender's record for all purposes.

CHAPTER 4

The Challenge of Inequality

The extent of our freedoms, the state of our politics, and the adequacy of our political institutions are essential topics in any discussion of liberalism. Underlying them is a broad question about the kind of society to which we aspire, and central to answering this question is the issue of equality. Crick recognized this in writing that politics must provide "conditions for deliberate social change by which groups can come to feel that they have an equitable stake in the prosperity and survival of the community."[1]

Proponents of liberalism acknowledge the importance of equality, but some critics say the goal has not been met and may be unrealizable in a liberal social order. Almost a half-century ago, the University of Toronto's C.B. Macpherson wrote about "the limits and possibilities of liberal democracy" in which he suggested that the continuance of liberal democracy depends on a down-grading of its capitalist assumptions and an upgrading of its liberal val-ues.[2] Macpherson's thesis was that there is incompatibility between liberal democracy conceived as "a society striv-ing to ensure that all its members are equally free to real-ize their capabilities"[3] and liberal democracy understood as "the democracy of a capitalist market society (no matter how modified that society appears to be by the rise of the welfare state)."[4] Contradictions between them, he argued, meant a growing unlikelihood that capitalism and liberal democracy could co-exist.

Macpherson was drawn to the possibility of participa-tory democracy, and he asked the question: "[c]an liberal democratic government be more participatory and, if so, how?"[5] He did not foresee direct democracy in large and complex modern societies; he recognized that these societies need elected politicians and continued reliance on indirect democracy. "The problem," he wrote, "is to make the elected politicians responsible,"[6] a task that required prerequisites, including a reduction in the social and economic inequality that is a barrier to a broadly participatory politics.[7] He saw openings through which this might be attained,[8] though he was not optimistic about the prospect.

In his 2004 book *The Collapse of Liberalism*, Charles Noble addressed a similar theme from an American perspective.[9] Unlike Macpherson, he celebrated capitalism: "a wondrous machine that has carried human societies to previously unimagined wealth.... No other economic system, no mat-ter how lofty its ambitions, has come close."[10] Capitalism and free markets "have also helped usher in and sustain fundamental political changes, widening the scope both of personal freedom and political democracy."[11] No society, he argues, has been able to create and maintain political democracy without first establishing and securing a market capitalist system."[12]

But, Noble wrote, "unfettered capitalism produces great inequities"[13] and needs the political left to achieve greater fairness. He observed that the average American "worries about the growing divide between the rich and poor"[14] and believes in equality of opportunity and equal respect.[15] He notes that Americans are not "radical egalitarians"[16] bent on redistributing income and wealth: only a minority believes that government has a responsibility to reduce income differences between high-income and low-income people.[17] For Noble, the way forward is to explain and defend the idea that "capitalism cannot work well without active government."[18] The agenda for active government must include electoral reform ("so that big money no longer dictates who runs and who wins and how incumbent politicians vote"[19]); campaign finance reform to end the money chase[20]; reining in corporate power to facilitate greater worker participation in decision-making and to make corporations more broadly accountable beyond their shareholders; a revived labour movement; and media reform. Though he found the current political situation "depressing,"[21] Noble saw hope for serious reform via "an active government in the service of greater opportunity and security."[22]

In 2012, Joseph Stiglitz offered what he called a snapshot of America's inequality: "[t]he simple story of America is this: the rich are getting richer, the richest of the rich are getting still richer, the poor are becoming poorer and more numerous, and the middle class is being hollowed out. The incomes of the middle class are stagnating or falling, and the difference between them and the truly rich is increasing."[23] The University of Montreal's John Peters argues that the Canadian experience is similar to that of the United States. In his 2022 volume *Jobs with Inequality*, he writes that, in recent decades, "income inequality has skyrocketed in Canada while the incomes of average households have deteriorated and the job quality for the majority of workers has plummeted. Indeed, in contrast to the view of Canada's economy as relatively equitable, Canada has instead closely followed trends in the United States, with inequality increasing in lockstep with the boom of the rich and super rich."[24]

A different perspective comes from McGill University economist William Watson in *The Inequality Trap: Fighting Capitalism Instead of Poverty*.[25] Watson writes: "if we respond to growing inequality by fighting capitalism, our false enemy, instead of poverty, our true enemy, we may end up with more of both inequality and poverty and risk at least partly undoing the good accrued during these past, truly remarkable two and a half centuries."[26] Between 1820, "which some economic historians regard as the beginning of globalized capitalism, and 2010, GDP per capita increased 17-fold in Western Europe, 23-fold in the 'western offshoots' (Canada, the United States and Australia), 17-fold in East Asia, 12-fold in Latin America and the Caribbean, 10-fold in the Middle East and North Africa, and 13-fold for the world on average."[27] And, we should add, it is not a coincidence that over roughly the same period we saw a rapid increase in life expectancy worldwide, nearly double, and "the greatest single achievement in history," according to American economist Julian Simon.[28]

The range of opinion points to a need for caution with respect to generalizations and comparisons on income inequality. It does not follow from market income comparisons alone that there is an ever-widening gap between and among different income groups. Different measures must be taken into account: market income; total income, including government transfers to households; and after-tax income under Canada's progressive tax system. Adjustments for inflation must be made, and wealth from all sources, including real estate, must be included. Over the past decade there has been an overall increase in the net worth of Canadians across income groups.[29]

A 2022 Bank of Canada discussion paper observes that "income inequality in the United States has been persistently higher than that in Canada for the past four decades," and that "Canada's income inequality increased substantially during the 1980s and first half of the 1990s but has been stable over the past 25 years."[30] Wealthy and very wealthy people attract attention in both countries. Recent measures identify forty-one Canadian billionaires and 514 centi-millionaires (people with at least US$100 million in investable assets), eighth in the world behind the United States, China, India, the United Kingdom, Germany, Switzerland, and Japan (in that order).[31] The super-rich in Canada should not receive as much attention as they do; they may attract curiosity, envy, resentment, or esteem depending on the perspective or political leanings of the observer, but their numbers do not make them a major benchmark for comparative purposes.

Income inequality is prominent in our consciousness because of daily reminders of differences in our capacities to acquire goods and services, and we know that income inequality at the lower end undermines participation in society in ways that we associate with a good life. However, equality of opportunity is the most frequently cited definition of equality. Stated without explanation or context, the concept does not take us far; its arguable meanings are many and range from an absence of discrimination to mandating identical resources. Legal philosopher and liberal theorist Ronald Dworkin approaches equality with "a general account of political obligation, of what a state, in particular, owes to its citizens."[32] Government, he argues, must treat its subjects with dignity and it lacks political legitimacy if it fails to do so: "Government must treat each and every person over whom it claims dominion with an equal concern and an equal respect."[33] Equal concern means that:

> social policy must take the fate of each individual to be equally important with the fate of any other. So, when deciding on a political policy, it can't discount the effect on some citizens. Obviously it can't do that because of their race, but it can't do that because of their economic class either. Equal respect is a rather different requirement. Equal respect means that government must respect the dignity of each individual by allowing each individual to determine for himself or herself what would count as a good life. What counts as a successful life.[34]

For Dworkin, this means that a theory of economic equality

> must reach an economic distribution which, at once, treats
> everyone's fate with equal concern, and respects people's
> responsibility to make their own decisions. This cannot be
> done by achieving flat equality. It can't be done by running
> the community as a monopoly game in which all the money
> gets taken in and redistributed at the end of each year. It can't
> do that because that would be to make individual decisions
> about education, investment, leisure, completely pointless.[35]

But we can't leave it only to the market because some people
are disadvantaged in the market for reasons they do not control. So, the question Dworkin asks is: "[h]ow do we treat
people both with equal concern and respect equally their
responsibility to make decisions for themselves?"[36] We don't
do this after the fact, he argues, "after fate has decided whose
investments mature and whose don't, whose education succeeds and whose doesn't, because that ... would make it
impossible to respect people's responsibility for their own
lives." We must provide for equality before the fact.[37]

Dworkin's answer to his own question is through a tax
and redistribution system with a hypothetical insurance
component. His answer has attracted support and criticism[38]
but is not our focus here. It is his framework of analysis:
the emphasis on equal concern and respect, and the integra-
tion of them in forward-looking social and fiscal policy, that
interests us. Equality of opportunity is advanced by access
to social capital, "a positive product of human interaction.
The positive outcome may be tangible or intangible and

may include favors, useful information, innovative ideas and future opportunities. Social capital is not held by an individual, but instead appears in the potential between social network connections between individuals."[39]

Harvard University's Robert Putnam wrote in 2004 that social capital in the United States had been seriously depleted in the previous thirty years. "By virtually every measure, today's Americans are more disconnected from one another and from the institutions of civic life than at any time since statistics have been kept."[40] In 2014, Hugh Segal and Carolyn Hughes Tuohy wrote that "the stock of social capital in Canada is different from that in the U.S.,"[41] and they cite our institutions and programs, attitudes towards government, universal health insurance, equalization, the child tax credit, and other examples in support of their claim.[42] But, they warn, Canadians must resist complacency: "the fact is that gaps in the life chances of upper-and lower-income kids exist in Canada … [t]hree million Canadians live in poverty – among them hundreds of thousands of children…. Our city neighborhoods across Canada are increasingly divided on a host of social and economic dimensions," while rural Canadians and First Nations[43] are particularly disadvantaged.[44] The direct and indirect costs of this are incalculable, and a renewed quest to end child poverty should be an urgent priority on our public policy agenda.

We have reached the point of recognizing that equal opportunity means wide availability of opportunities to secure a good life with concerted attention to improving those chances for disadvantaged people, particularly children at or near poverty levels. Supportive social programs and strong social capital are important components of equal opportunity; underlying them is a requirement that robust economic performance is necessary to improve and sustain them, a sorely neglected subject in Canadian public discourse. In 2020, economist Don Drummond wrote that "Canada needs a national debate over its economic and fiscal future.... We have been locked into a path of mediocre productivity and real income gains for far too long."[45] Former finance minister Bill Morneau shared Drummond's concern in writing that his time in government convinced him that "productivity improvement is the most important issue on our agenda"[46] and it is not receiving the attention it requires. Competitiveness, weak business investment, poor growth forecasts, lagging performance in developing and exploiting intellectual property, an equalization program in need of reform[47] – all point to a vulnerable Canadian economy, and that is before the economic costs of the pandemic and of climate change are worked into the equation. Government leaders gloss over these issues in public, citing only what they see as reports and data that paint a more positive picture, and they are virtually absent from wide public discussion in Parliament and elsewhere. The message here is simple: improving and sustaining equality requires a healthy economy, and we need to pay more attention to this requirement.

We turn now to equality under the Charter and, in particular, to sections 15 and 1:

15(1) Every individual is equal before and under the law and has the right to equal protection and equal benefit of the law without discrimination and, in particular, without discrimination based on race, national or ethnic origin, colour, religion, sex, age or mental or physical disability.

15(2) Subsection (1) does not preclude any law, program or activity that has as its object the amelioration of conditions of disadvantaged individuals or groups including those that are disadvantaged because of race, national or ethnic origin, colour, religion, sex, age or mental or physical disability.

1. The Canadian Charter of Rights and Freedoms guarantees the rights and freedoms set out in it subject only to such reasonable limits prescribed by law as can be demonstrably justified in a free and democratic society.

Section 24(1) provides redress: 'Anyone whose rights or freedoms, as guaranteed by this Charter, have been infringed or denied may apply to a court of competent jurisdiction to obtain such remedy as the court considers appropriate and just in the circumstances.'

Section 15 is at once constitutional assurance that individuals are equal before the law and free of discrimination, and recognition that they may be discriminated against in the implementation of affirmative action programs. The provisions apply to federal, provincial, and municipal governments, and a threshold question in considering their ambit is whether they have wider application. The question has been litigated, and we learn from *Eldridge v. British Columbia (Attorney-General)*[48] that an entity subject to extensive government control may be deemed to be a part of government, with the Charter applying to all of its activities, or an entity not part of government that implements specified government policies or programs may fall under the Charter with respect to those policies or programs. Universities are an example; they are not controlled by government, but they discharge government policies with respect to post-secondary education and so may engage the Charter with respect to those policies.[49]

We take, as an example, the University of Calgary's 2022 cluster hiring initiative whereby forty-five professors to be hired in three subsequent years must be from equity-deserving groups: women, Indigenous peoples, visual/racialized minorities, persons with disabilities, and LGBTQ2S persons. It is clear that white males who are neither LGBTQ2S nor disabled need not apply because the cluster initiative will exclude them from consideration regardless of their academic standing and competitiveness in qualifications and achievements. Public university faculty appointments would arguably fall under the Charter because they are part of the province's policies relating to post-secondary instruction.

On its face, the U of C cluster initiative denies the right to equality and freedom from discrimination to white males who are neither disabled nor LGBTQ2S with the consequence that they are barred from applying for forty-five jobs at a public university supported in part by their tax dollars. The university's claim is that this an exercise of university equity, diversity, and inclusion (EDI) policies aimed at historically disadvantaged groups and, accordingly, is not precluded under Charter section 15(2). In response to this claim, we might look to EDI definitions offered by the University of Toronto:

> Equity is the promotion of fairness and justice for each indi-
> vidual that considers historical, social, systemic and struc-
> tural issues that impact experience and individual needs.
> Diversity is a measure of representation within a commu-
> nity or population that includes identity, background, lived
> experience, culture and many more. Inclusion is the creation
> of an environment where everyone shares a sense of belong-
> ing, is treated with respect, and is able to fully participate.[50]

Notably, this definition of equity focuses on individuals, not
groups, and it is individual equality rights that are fundamental in liberal societies. Section 15(2) provides that these
equality rights do not preclude affirmative action programs;
it does not mean that programs so described pre-empt equality rights. In the words of the University of Toronto's definition of EDI, "fairness and justice for each individual" within
or outside the disadvantaged groups, requires that each
individual's case be evaluated on merit. In some cases, fairness and justice may require positive consideration of their
membership in one or more of the disadvantaged groups; in
other cases, not so. The University of Calgary's cluster initiative goes much further than this. It excludes men of white
skin colour who are neither LGBTQ2S nor disabled from
applying for forty-five positions; there is no opportunity for
them to compete with other applicants for these positions.
The university claims that this advances diversity and inclusion, but rights are individual and the paradox inescapable:
for ineligible white males, it is exclusionary.

In her 2020 volume *Faces of Inequality: A Theory of Wrongful Discrimination*,[51] the University of Toronto's Sophia

Moreau helps us understand wrongful discrimination. Her deep study, rooted in philosophy and law, offers ideas that are materiel here. It seems that she would view our example of the University of Calgary cluster initiative as one of direct discrimination which "consists of an act or a practice that explicitly singles out a person or group that possesses a certain trait and treats them less favourably than others because of that trait."[52] White-skinned potential applicants for the forty-five U of C posts who are neither LGBTQ2S nor disabled are ineligible to apply for them and are thereby treated less favourably (unequally) than applicants from the equity groups identified in the policy. The initiative's defenders may argue that ineligible whites enjoy off-setting advantages which qualifies their right to equality, but Moreau would not agree. She argues that a society of equals is not a society in which we are all equally well off weighing disadvantages in some contexts against advantages in others. Rather, it is a society in which no one has to endure certain kinds of disadvantage even if they enjoy advantages elsewhere.[53] This does not conclude the issue of discrimination for Moreau; she acknowledges that while the state is always under a duty to treat its citizens as equals, "it may sometimes be justified in violating that duty."[54] But the bar is high. The state's duty to treat its citizens as equals is a constitutive duty, one that is central to "a country whose people are committed to live as equals."[55] She writes that "it is arguable that it can only be justifiable for the state to violate this duty in cases where it can appeal to the need to fulfill some other constitutive duty – some other duty that, like the duty to treat everyone as equals, grows out of the very purpose of having a state."[56] No other constitutive duty is present here.

Central to Moreau's views on affirmative action is the idea of deliberative freedom, "the freedom to deliberate about one's life and to decide what to do in light of those deliberations, without having to treat certain personal traits, or other people's assumptions about them, as costs and without having to live with these traits always before one's eyes."[57] She reminds us here of Dworkin's insistence that equal respect is a component of equality: "[e]qual respect means that government must respect the dignity of each individual by allowing each individual to determine for himself or herself what would count as a good life."[58] Affirmative action may lessen deliberative freedom by making race an obstacle in pursuit of a good life. This does not, for Moreau, rule out affirmative action, but it does imply that we must approach the subject with circumspection, taking into account the extent of deliberative freedom lost, the possible justifications for the deprivation, and that "it is implicit in such policies that they are temporary and remedial."[59]

Debate on affirmative action is not over. In the United States, it is now unconstitutional as a result of the Supreme Court decision in actions brought by Students for Fair Admissions, Inc. against Harvard College and the University of North Carolina[60] in which it was alleged that the two universities' admissions policies violated the US Fourteenth Amendment. Chief Justice John Roberts wrote the majority opinion in the Students' favour with the nine judges divided along the perceived right-left lines in the Court:

six–three in the North Carolina case, and six–two in the Harvard decision, with Justice Ketanji Brown Jackson recusing herself because of her previous service on the university's Board of Overseers. The case is the latest decision on the US Fourteenth Amendment, which forbids state denial of equal protection of the laws to any person. The Amendment came into force in the aftermath of the US Civil War, and its guarantee of equal protection "was circumvented for many decades by the post-Reconstruction-era black codes, Jim Crow laws, and the U.S. Supreme Court's "separate but equal" ruling in *Plessy v. Ferguson*."[61] This early legacy was gradually eroded in the years that followed and reversed in 1954 when a unanimous Supreme Court ruled in *Brown v. Board of Education*[62] that racial segregation in public schools was a violation of the Fourteenth Amendment. With this commitment to equal protection, the question soon asked was whether actions could be taken to address historic inequalities by affirmative action, including race-conscious admissions policies in universities. The answer provided by the Supreme Court in subsequent cases was yes, but with important qualifications that emphasized the primacy of the equal protection clause. It applies "without regard to any differences of race, of color, or of nationality – it is universal in its application."[63] Further, "[a]ny exceptions to the Equal Protection clause's guarantee must survive a daunting two-step examination known as 'strict scrutiny,' ... which asks first whether the racial classification is used 'to further compelling governmental interests,' ... and second whether the governments use of race is 'narrowly tailored,' i.e. necessary to achieve that interest."[64]

The Regents of the University of California v. Bakke[65] was the landmark decision on affirmative action, and Justice Powell's opinion in that case became "the touchstone for constitutional analysis of race-conscious admissions policies."[66] He observed: "[t]he guarantee of equal protection cannot mean one thing when applied to one individual and something else when applied to a person of another color."[67] He did not find the university's justifications for race-based admissions compelling, except for its claim that education is enriched by a racially diverse student body. This did not allow universities the freedom to do as they liked in race-conscious policies: "[r]acial and ethnic distinctions of any sort are inherently suspect ... and antipathy toward them was deeply rooted in our Nation's constitutional and demographic history."[68]

Accordingly, a university could not employ a two-track quota system with a specific number of seats for individuals from a preferred ethnic group. Neither still could a university use race to foreclose an individual from all consideration. Race could only operate as a plus in a particular applicant's file, and even then it had to be weighed in a manner flexible enough to consider all pertinent elements of diversity in light of the particular qualifications of each applicant.[69]

Moreover, as the subsequent Supreme Court case of *Grutter v. Bollinger*[70] confirmed, race-conscious admissions programs must be limited in time. If they are doing what was intended they should in due course no longer be necessary.

It was against this background that the Harvard and North Carolina cases were addressed. The majority, led by Chief Justice Roberts, held that the two universities ran afoul of the restrictions by which race-based admissions were to be managed: "[u]niversity programs must comply with strict scrutiny, they may never use race as a stereotype or negative, and – at some point they must end. Respondents admissions systems ... fail each of these criteria."[71] The Court did not think these failures remediable. The goals set out by the universities were "standard less"[72]; the racial categories they used were imprecise, arbitrary, undefined, or inconclusive; and it was clear that the universities contemplated no end to their race-based admissions programs. To the universities' argument that they are owed deference on these programs, the Court acknowledged that some deference was historically given but "only within constitutionally prescribed limits."[73] The Court held their programs "cannot be reconciled with the guarantees of the Equal Protection Clause."[74] It did not rule out altogether the consideration of race in admissions decisions: "nothing in this opinion should be construed as prohibiting universities from considering an applicant's discussion of how race affected his or her life, be it through discrimination, inspiration or otherwise."[75] But the decision ends affirmative action as it evolved since the decision in Bakke.

What does the decision mean for Canada? Affirmative action is alive and well in this country and enjoys constitutional protection, but this should not lead us to dismiss the Harvard and North Carolina cases only as an example of the growing divergence between Canada and the United States.

The tension between individual rights and affirmative action is experienced in Canada too, and how it is resolved matters to Canadians. Section 15(1) of the Charter articulates the core principle: equality of individual Canadians before and under the law and the right to equal protection and equal benefit of the law. Section 15(2) recognizes that programs may be necessary to address disadvantaged individuals or groups in the interest of ensuring their equality with other Canadians. When these programs diminish individual rights of those who are not their beneficiaries, they must be carefully scrutinized to ensure their compatibility with the equality of all Canadians. The question of whether the programs are necessary and whether they are appropriately "tailored" to reach their goals should be asked and answered – by the courts.

We return to the example of the University of Calgary cluster hiring initiative, which excludes white applicants who are neither LGBTQ2S nor disabled from the candidate pools for forty-five professorships regardless of their academic qualifications. Was this sweeping disqualification needed? Is the cluster initiative appropriately tailored to defensible objectives? The questions themselves demonstrate the need for more judicial scrutiny of affirmative action initiatives. To reference again an issue in the Harvard and North Carolina cases, our courts should not defer to universities in these matters. As Justice Roberts said, the universities' appeal to "just trust us" is not a good enough answer to the issues at stake,[76] – not in the United States and not in Canada either.

One further observation by Moreau requires our attention: "it is implicit in [affirmative action] policies that they are temporary and remedial."[77] The writer's experience is in line with this observation, but more recent experience may not be. Many Canadian universities have established EDI offices as permanent offices in their administrations. They are often led by vice-provosts and have growing numbers of employees in their offices. With a race-based calculus of employees at hand, they monitor racial demographics in order to align workforce numbers with them. Their focus may be on the underrepresented, but they may encounter overrepresentation too. What then? Do they propose measures to reduce numbers larger than they think there should be? The questions are hypothetical, but they point to a risk of affirmative action measures that may not be temporary and remedial; rather, they may be ongoing adjustments of people and policies according to race. If we are heading in this direction, we may anticipate greater race-based resentment and anger. The answer is to restore the right to equality and freedom from discrimination to the lead in diversity discussions and to welcome court challenges to measures seen to be excessive or repressive.

Conclusion

This chapter began with a reference to C.B. Macpherson's scepticism about liberal democracy as a capitalist market society and liberal democracy striving to achieve equal opportunity for its members. It is a scepticism that endures among those who believe that the days of western liberalism are numbered, though we have heard the contrary argument that market economies and striving for equality are not only compatible; market economies are integral to democracies and the value they place on equality. It seems that the differences may be rooted more in contrasting definitions of equality than in differences about the fate of western economies. The view here is that equality and equality rights are fundamental to liberalism, and their defence is a necessary part of Anne Applebaum's "ferocious fight"[78] to ensure the survival of liberal societies.

The mention of equality invites the question "equality in what?" and this chapter includes discussion of income equality, equality of opportunity, equality rights, freedom from discrimination, and affirmative action. Whole treatises have been written on these subjects, and their treatment here is brief and incomplete, but it leads to these observations:

- Income inequalities and equality of opportunity require particular attention to children in poverty and Indigenous communities. More than a million Canadian children live in poverty,[79] at inestimable cost to them and to our country's future. New policies with measurable goals should be established to reduce and eliminate child poverty.
- Indigenous communities will continue to need major investments in safe drinking water, better housing, and improved opportunities for their peoples. The issues here are well documented, though the political context is uncertain[80] and progress has been gradual.
- Equality requires, in Ronald Dworkin's words, that governments accord equal concern and equal respect to all

citizens. Equal concern means that "social policy must
take the fate of each individual to be equally important
with the fate of any other.... Equal respect means that
government must respect the dignity of each individual
by allowing each individual to determine for himself or
herself what would count as a good life."[81]

- Equality of opportunity means the wide availability of
opportunities to secure a good life. A successful economy and strong middle class are prerequisites to these
opportunities, and they are further advanced by strong
social capital.

- Section 15 of the Charter is at once constitutional assurance that Canadians enjoy equality before the law and
freedom from discrimination and recognition that they
may be discriminated against in affirmative action policies. Affirmative action policies should be monitored
to determine, as Sophia Moreau suggests, the extent of
the deliberative freedom lost in affirmative action, the
justifications for the loss, and whether affirmative action
policies are temporary and remedial.

- The chosen example of the University of Calgary cluster hiring initiative is illiberal in the sweeping freedom
loss caused to potential white applicants for forty-five
academic positions. Its justification is not articulated,
and it appears to be only one initiative in likely ongoing
affirmative action based on racial demographics. Hopefully it will be challenged by one or more of the inevita-
bly unsuccessful white applicants for these jobs.

CHAPTER 5

Expectations of Democracy: Institutions, Trust, and Accountability

Public opinion polls are a constant in our lives, sometimes reflecting matters that quickly pass across our overloaded attention spans, other times informing us about issues of greater import. Among the latter is a Postmedia-Leger national poll published early in 2023 which reports that most Canadians believe that the country is broken.[1] A majority in all regions, and a two-thirds majority overall, agree with the sentiment, and it should not be dismissed as a transitory vignette that will fade as new issues capture our attention. To repeat Peter Newman's phrase in another context, there is a distemper of our times[2] – a caustic, polarizing quality in our public discourse, and diminishing tolerance for the differences that are inevitable in a large and diverse country. From our leaders to people on the street, we hear little of pride in Canada and optimism about its future.

McMaster University's Janet Ajzenstat writes that "[g]loomy thoughts about the future of liberal democracy are the order of the day,"[3] and that "cynicism, anger and apathy prevail."[4] The sentiments are not limited to Canada, but they are common here and lead us to reflect upon our expectations of Canadian democracy, and in particular our institutions. Canadians know little about them and some – including the current prime minister – dismiss them in negative, ahistorical terms.[5] But it is our institutions that hold the country together, and if the hold is weakening, the country's future is imperilled. Ajzenstat's focus is on Canada's Parliament, and she is positive about its origins. She explores the influence of Enlightenment thinkers, the discussions in Charlottetown, Quebec City, and London, and also what she calls Canada's ratification debates: "the debates on Confederation in the parliaments and assemblies of the British North American colonies."[6] These debates "show us political men of the Confederation period drawing on Locke, Burke and other sources in the history of philosophy to support, challenge and illustrate concrete political prescriptions."[7]

The result, Ajzenstat argues, is "an excellent example of an Enlightenment constitution," a durable constitution with an unexcelled record in protecting the equal right to life and liberty; not perfect but none better.[8] The University of Saskatchewan's David E. Smith would have agreed: "Canada has one of the world's most enduring and successful constitutions. It is among a handful of countries that existed in 1914 and retain the same form of government as then."[9] Consequently, we do not need to rework the constitution; we need to make it work. Ajzenstat quotes Michael Ignatieff: "What we need is a reinvigoration of the institutions of freedom ... Reinvigoration means simply that our institutions need to do the job that they were designed to do. We need to understand what they are there for, trust in them, and make them work."[10]

Canada's Parliament consists of the House of Commons, the Senate, and the Crown. In determining what is required to make our institutions work, we turn first to Donald J. Savoie's *Democracy in Canada: The Disintegration of our Institutions*.[11] Savoie's thesis is that Canada has the building blocks of representative democracy – political parties, a free press, a professional public service, and an independent judiciary – but that they are not up to the task.[12] There are, he writes, four major challenges:

> First, the country's national political institutions remain unable to both address the regional factor in shaping policy and to operate under constitutional conventions that underpin Westminster parliamentary government. Second, government bureaucracy has lost its way, and it is no longer able to meet the expectations of politicians and citizens. Third, the average citizen believes that national political institutions cater to those who serve in them, to economic elites, and to interest groups at their expense. Fourth, accountability in government no longer meets present-day requirements given the rise of the new media, the work of lobbyists, and incessant calls for greater transparency.[13]

Savoie is not alone in his negative assessment. In 2020 journalist Jonathan Manthorpe wrote that "Canada has a serious

democratic deficit."[14] Particularly telling is his observation
that "Parliament and the legislatures have become largely
devoid of relevance as venues for the debate and resolution
of issues facing the country."[15] Savoie helps us understand
why: the decline of the House of Commons "and the role of
MPs, particularly over the past forty years, has been well
documented."[16] The "golden rules" for newly elected members who hope to advance their careers are: follow party dis-
cipline, do not raise contentious issues in public, and don't
create problems for the party leader.[17] When toe the line is
the order of the day, we cannot expect MPs to bring substance to public discourse.

We might expect that members of cabinet – those chosen
to lead ministries – might compensate for the decline in the
role of MPs, but Savoie's verdict is blunt: "cabinet government is failing."[18] One former minister contends that "cabinet is not a decision-making body, it is a focus group for the
prime minister."[19] Cabinet does not make policy; it does not
make important decisions; and it has failed, in recent years,
to represent the country's regions.[20]

The Canadian Senate "has confronted a crisis of legitimacy for much of its existence."[21] The fact that members are
appointed, not elected, is at the heart of the problem, though
proponents of an elected Senate often overlook the question of how an elected upper chamber would align with the
rest of the constitution. Devoting "sober second thought"
to House of Commons deliberations and serving as a voice
of regional interests and of underrepresented minorities are
worthy mandates, and the Senate has generally met the first
of these in reviewing legislation without incurring credible

charges of obstruction. Its service to regions and under-represented minorities are more difficult to assess, though unequal membership across provinces and regions under-mines its credibility and effectiveness. Recent changes in the appointments process in favour of independent sena-tors have reduced partisanship and improved the quality of appointments, but the underrepresentation of the four western provinces, particularly in comparison to the Atlan-tic provinces, remains a major weakness. With a combined population of nearly 12 million, Alberta, B.C., Manitoba, and Saskatchewan have twenty-four Senate seats, six for each province. With a combined population of 2.4 million, Atlantic Canada has thirty seats, ten in each of New Bruns-wick and Nova Scotia, six in Newfoundland and Labrador, and four in Prince Edward Island. It is remarkable that the country has not found a way to address such a clear and striking imbalance.

With the increasing centralization of power in the prime minister's office, and with it – in Savoie's words, a failing cabinet government – a diminished public service is an inevitable result. Anyone whose work intersects with gov-ernment understands the importance of the public service, whether in service delivery or in accessing decision-makers. Public servants know the sectors in which they work, the people who work in them, and they understand the con-text in which decisions must be made. But "[s]enior pub-lic servants have been on the defensive for the past forty years or more. Since the early 1980's, public servants have been told that they do not measure up to their private sec-tor counterparts.... In short, the verdict from politicians has been that public servants are not up to task on either policy or managing government operations."[22] It is a damning verdict on the hundreds of thousands of federal public servants, not to mention comparable numbers of their provincial counterparts.

Fortunately, these issues are not beyond reach. Savoie concludes:

> Political will, not constitutional amendments, can reinstate the House of Commons's role as the "legitimator," or the only legitimate voice that can speak for all of Canada's communities, and can turn the Senate into the voice of the regions. Political will is all that is needed to make the Cabinet the government's policy-making body, where all important issues are brought for resolution rather than serving as a body to simply ratify decisions taken by prime ministers and their courtiers. Political will is all that is required to give the public service authoritative judgment, a renewed capacity to develop and put forward evidence-based advice, as well as a capacity to deliver programs and services efficiently.[23]

Savoie's observations are reminiscent of Ajzenstat and Ignatieff: we don't have to rework government; we have to make government work.

The Crown is part of Parliament, and many Canadians think of it as an ornamental feature that could easily be detached from Parliament without disruption to the wider government apparatus. Wide admiration for Elizabeth II may have deferred the question of the monarchy's future in Canada, though with her passing we can expect the issue to be raised again. Despite considerable ambivalence on the subject, a majority favours discontinuing the monarchy in favour of a republican alternative.[24]

The question – monarchy or republic – is more complicated than is commonly supposed. In *Canada's Deep Crown*[25] the three authors contend that "the Crown has been a fundamental contributing influence in creating a country and a constitution whose distinctive characteristics embrace, among other matters, the promotion of political moderation, societal accommodation, adaptable constitutional structures, as well as governing practices that favour cultural and linguistic pluralism."[26] The Crown is a symbol, one that is pervasive in our system of government, and its acknowledged prerogatives are not exercised by a monarch in London but by a Canadian vice-regal family of eleven members – the governor general and lieutenant governors for each province. Far from being a colonial artefact, it is a modern institution of Parliament whose role rests on "an amorphous combination of legal rules, constitutional conventions, historical practices, and tacit understandings and arrangements."[27] Moreover, "the Crown today in Canada … is now deeply, almost permanently protected."[28] Changes to the office of the King, the Governor General, and the Lieutenant Governor of a province require consent of all legislative assemblies in the country.[29]

The Crown is embedded in our history and is a central feature of our evolution as a nation. "In contrast to the United States, which had a revolutionary break with the British Crown, Canada retained and embraced the Crown, achieving independence through agreements about how the

Crown would behave, rather than casting it off in favour of a republican form of government."[30] While our attention may often be drawn to the personalities at Buckingham Palace, the "celebrity status of the sovereign and members of the Royal Family end up distracting us from the nature and function of the Crown as the load-bearing structure of an entire system of government."[31] We may contemplate sentiment that the king of the United Kingdom should no longer be king of Canada, though a change here would require a constitutional amendment, but it is the questions "why" and "what next?" that should give us pause. So far, there have been no compelling answers to these questions, which suggests that constitutional monarchy continues to serve us better than the imagined alternatives.

From our institutions, our focus shifts to the related subjects of trust and accountability. Former Governor General David Johnston writes:

> Trust is the bedrock of democracy. Democracy – in Canada and in countries around the world – depends on a rule of law that strives toward justice. That rule of law depends on trust – a trust in each other as citizens, and a trust between citizens and the institutions that stand for and serve them.[32]

This trust is badly frayed. The Edelman Trust Barometer measures trust in government, business, NGOs, and media across twenty-eight countries, including Canada; business fares better than the other three, but overall the study documents "[a] lack of faith in societal institutions triggered by economic anxiety, disinformation, mass-class divide and a failure of leadership," resulting in "a deeply dangerous and polarized" world.[33] Proof Inc., a Canadian firm, also measures trust with results comparable to the Edelman study, though particularly disturbing is the finding that in 2023 only "49 per cent of Canadians ... trust their country to perform as a democracy, down 16 per cent from 65 per cent in 2020."[34] We can be encouraged that "new Canadians continue to be more trusting than their fellow citizens,"[35] but, in general, the evidence tells us that Canadians have diminished trust in one another as citizens and in our public institutions.

The problem is exacerbated by regional and provincial distrust across boundaries in this vast country, though most serious is declining trust in an institution that is at the centre of democratic life – the electoral system. A March 2023 Leger Poll found that 29 per cent of Canadians rate our electoral system as unsafe,[36] not an alarming number except in a historical context in which questions about the integrity of the system were virtually unheard. No doubt the number is influenced by recent history in the United States, which is further down the track in distrust of elections, and by reports of Chinese interference in our elections, but it remains troubling and should be monitored in hopes that it turns upward and not further down.

The former governor general writes: "[p]ublic institutions can stabilize and restore trust by showing they value the solid, valid information that makes it possible for our democracy not only to operate properly but to survive."[37] Canadian governments – federal and provincial – have freedom of information legislation, and they extol transparency and compliance measures on their websites, but one study describes our system as broken.[38] In a twenty-month investigation called Secret Canada, *The Globe and Mail* conducted hundreds of interviews, analysed thousands of records and appeal decisions, and audited freedom of information statistics and practices. Their study "has shown that – at a time of plummeting trust in governments and institutions – every day, public bodies and governments are breaking the law."[39] Across Canada, the study reports:

> FOI units have been starved of resources and staff. Institutions can no longer meet their statutory deadlines. The laws themselves are impractical in a digital world. And it is normal for institutions to refuse to release records that judges and adjudicators have repeatedly said are public, such as government contracts.[40]

Globe editor-in-chief David Walmsley concludes: "[o]ur freedom of information systems, binding networks to ensure Canadians have transparency, have collapsed under their own weight."[41]

In addition to a broken information system, there is concern that transparency and accountability may not be deliverable because of other institutional shortcomings, interest groups and their lobbyists, and social media. Canadians' observations of behaviours of their leaders and others in public life suggest they perceive excessive levels of spin and obfuscation. Question Period in the House of Commons is an opportunity to hold government to account, though opportunities to do so are fewer because the number of sitting days has declined[42] and the event itself has descended into theatre in which "[s]cripted performances are the norm, interrupted by heckling and raucous partnership. Performance trumps substance, conflict conquers collaboration and controlled messaging subsumes organic debate."[43]

Interest group activity is growing. These are groups organized around shared interests that seek to influence those who make or help shape public policy by moving them in the direction of their preferred outcomes. They are inevitable in government and may be constructive in policy formation, but there are potential negatives too. "Interest group influence, if opaque and disproportionate, may lead to administrative bribery, political corruption, undue influence and state capture."[44] There are thousands of federal lobbyists in Canada,[45] and to reduce the negative risks, the country regulates the activity. Overseen by a commissioner of lobbying with investigatory powers, Canada has a Lobbying Act, which requires that lobbyists be registered, report on their activities, and adhere to a code of conduct; failure to comply with the act is an offence punishable by fine or imprisonment or both.[46] Provinces have similar legislation.

The high number of registered lobbyists is evidence of compliance, but the full extent of the activity across the country is unknown. Unpaid lobbyists are not covered by the legislation; nor are the increasing numbers of special interest groups whose unpaid adherents exert strong and sometimes loud pressure on members of Parliament. "Free and open access to government" is an underlying principle of the Lobbying Act,[47] but public perception is important here. A problem remains if paid or unpaid lobbying is seen as privileged access to government that sometimes carries the day against the better interests of Canadians.

Decline of traditional media has diminished trust in information. It was not long ago that large numbers of Canadians tuned into CBC's *The National* with Peter Mansbridge or *CTV News* with Lloyd Robertson to learn the day's news. They, and anchors before them, such as Knowlton Nash and Earl Cameron, were "our version of Canadian celebrities"[48] at a time when 80 per cent of North Americans learned the news from television.[49] They were "very important icons of a network's identity and integrity."[50] Canadians might have supplemented what they learned from television by reading one or more national or local newspapers that were seen as credible sources of information and opinion.

Now a process of massification in communications is underway and irreversible. With hundreds of channels, multiple networks, and a weakened print media, past news sources have diminishing presence and influence, and social media has fundamentally altered the origins of information available to us. Most of the earth's population have access to the internet, receive news from it, and many contribute their own versions of news, but with none of the standards, accountabilities, and constraints of the traditional media. The problem is compounded by AI-generated propaganda that can be expected to grow in the years to come.[51] Journalist and Nobel laureate Maria Ressa believes that "we have maybe two years to turn back the tide toward what she calls authoritarian technocracy (a form of government in which would-be dictators lead by manipulating public opinion online towards autocracy)."[52]

Conclusion

The impacts of social media require our concerted attention. Though still in their early stages, the prospects are identifiable and troubling. New York University's Jonathan Haidt describes "three major forces that collectively bind together successful democracies: social capital (extensive social networks with high levels of trust), strong institutions and shared stories."[53] Haidt's key message is that social media has weakened all three.[54] It is "corrosive to trust in governments, news media, and people and institutions in general."[55] Without major change he contemplates the collapse of American democracy (and Canadian democracy would not be far behind). He identifies three goals that must be achieved for democracy to survive: "[w]e must harden democratic institutions so that they can withstand chronic anger and mistrust, reform social media so that it becomes less socially corrosive, and better prepare the next generation for democratic citizenship in this new age."[56]

Canada's democratic institutions are not up to this challenge; they are not strong or trusted let alone hardened. To summarize what this chapter has documented: members of Parliament are expected to toe the line of party leadership in their activities and communications; the role of cabinet ministers is diminished by the centralized power of the prime minister and his political office; the Senate is seriously unrepresentative; the future of the Crown is uncertain; and federal public servants are undermined by criticism that they are not up to the tasks before them. A decline in trust is confirmed by Edelman, Proof Inc., and public opinion polls, and once-trusted sources of information are compromised as mass communication and social media grow. Reform of our institutions has become urgent and must include robust non-partisan discussion of the goals identified by Haidt. This discussion must come at the official level and not be driven by the shrill and intolerant voices that are so loud and common today.

The problems described above are formidable, though not beyond reach. We have learned that Canada has a strong, enduring constitution, and our history has many examples of Canadians rising to challenges before them. We shall need these examples again.

CHAPTER 6

Overview and Conclusion

There are two principal narratives on a struggle against illiberalism. One narrative holds that such a struggle is unnecessary, a preoccupation of conservatives and an expression of their resistance to a progressive agenda that is, on the whole, positive. Another is that illiberalism is a fact and a growing phenomenon and that it is a threat to liberal democracy. The argument in this volume is that the latter is the more compelling narrative.

There is a wide range of illiberal thinking. A vivid example at the time of this writing is a Health Canada Report prepared for the chief public health officer.[1] Ostensibly about climate change and public health, the three authors and their interviewees went further afield, blaming capitalism, Western society, colonialism, and white supremacy for both climate change and negative health outcomes. One of those they consulted added that liberty and individualism, too, are in the way of progress. The appeal came from three self-described uninvited white settlers who titled their work "What we Heard," an approach that frees them from demonstrating that what they heard is evidence-based, cogent, and compelling. Though far-out, their conclusions are explicitly threatening to the idea of Canada.

This is not the only example of talk about ending the market economy, the rule of law, and Western society. We may recall Janet Ajzenstat's observation that "[g]loomy thoughts about the future of liberal democracy are the order of the day,"[2] and a strand of Indigenous thought stipulates that the end of the market economy and rule of law are prerequisites to reconciliation.[3] The vulnerability of liberal democracy is recorded by Martin Wolf, who argues that the 2008–9 financial crisis followed by the rise of populism "has generated profound social, cultural and then political convulsions that threaten both democracy and capitalism. But the larger threat to democratic capitalism comes from within – with the decline of public trust in our democratic capitalist system and our institutions."[4] Demagogic leaders and followers have jumped into the gap. "In another time they would have been ignored or dismissed. The critical filtering function once provided by professional journalism has been supplanted by social media, which gives free access to anyone with a cause or complaint, the louder the better."[5] It will be further supplanted by artificial intelligence, which has an unlimited capacity to produce fake news and images.[6]

In answering the question "what is to be done?" we return to Anne Applebaum's call for a "ferocious fight" for liberalism – a call that recognizes that the voices of illiberalism are numerous and loud and that a concerted effort is required to counter them. In considering what this concerted effort might involve, we acknowledge components of illiberalism that are identified in this volume. In chapter one, we noted initiatives to tune out ideas by blocking or silencing guest speakers; using trigger warnings to forewarn individuals of potentially troubling ideas to which they may be exposed; burning books or culling titles deemed offensive from libraries, a recent example being what the Peel County School Board called an equity cull to take Anne Frank's diary off the bookshelves; shouting down voices thought to be objectionable. To these we add editing by 'sensitivity readers' to expunge potentially offensive language from books by Roald Dahl, Ian Fleming, Agatha Christie, and no doubt others to come. Freedom of expression in these and other ways is under attack.

In chapter two, we encountered the decline of Bernard Crick's vision of politics, and in particular the factors that led to its decline: ideology, populism, and turning away from reason and from the virtues that enable politics – prudence, tolerance, compromise, and adaptability. Ideological commitments foster polarization, and it is growing on both conservative and liberal sides of the Canadian political divide. Populism is a major force in our closest neighbour – the United States – and a presence in Canada too. Insistence on reason in our public lives is waning, as are the virtues that enable politics. In chapter three, we add hate to Crick's list, but we must distinguish between increasingly common and reckless attributions of hate that some people direct to those with whom they disagree and the real hate and hate crimes that are on the rise in the Western world.

Equality is an essential topic in any discussion of liberalism. Some critics have argued that liberalism falls short in implementing equality, though here we must distinguish between equal opportunity and equal outcomes. The former is an historically liberal understanding of equality; the latter emphasizes the same or similar treatment and results. They are archetypes: equality of opportunity requires that we foresee reasonable outcomes and, in general, equality of outcomes requires that gaps be narrowed, not strictly equal results. Clearly there is room for a broad range of opinion within and between the two archetypes.

Equality before and under the law is fundamental to liberalism and is guaranteed under section 15(1) of the Charter of Rights and Freedoms which outlaws discrimination based on race, national or ethnic origin, skin colour, religion, sex, or mental and physical disability. Section 15(2) qualifies the guarantee in providing that it does not preclude actions undertaken to ameliorate conditions of disadvantaged persons or groups. The language here is important; affirmative action programs are not precluded by section 15(1), but they are not accorded blanket exemption by 15(2). We considered the example of the University of Calgary's hiring cluster by which white persons who are neither disabled nor LGBTQ2S are barred from competing for forty-five professorships. It is argued in chapter four that the wide discrimination under the U of C initiative is unjustly discriminatory and should be challenged under section 15(1). The US Supreme Court decision on affirmative action discussed in chapter four would help in a challenge.

In chapter five, we noted flaws in our institutions and a lack of confidence and trust in them. Institutions that do not work well stand in the way of a fight against illiberalism, so we must include them in our discussion.

This volume claims that the threats to liberalism summarized above are real and substantial, and we must ask why they are not taken more seriously in mainstream debate. Perhaps because the claims are thought to be overblown, or because there are more voices advancing competing narratives, or because too many voices remain silent on the issues. Readers will judge whether the claims are overblown and competing narratives more persuasive, but they should consider again the consequences that befell some of those identified in this manuscript: individuals banned from campuses or who have endured campaigns to fire them; large numbers of university faculty who self-censor their political views for fear of retaliation by colleagues and students; white students discouraged from using a university lounge intended for non-whites; a graduate communications student interrogated and denounced by her supervisor and program head because she showed her students a debate in which Jordan Peterson was a participant, her Wilfrid Laurier University accusers odiously comparing him to Hitler; potential white applicants barred from seeking any of forty-five positions in a hiring cluster at a Canadian university; and school teachers fired or otherwise disciplined for taking issue with orthodoxies. Unchecked by liberal voices, these examples and others will multiply.

A constant in our struggle against illiberalism must be a push back against identity politics. Philosopher Susan

Neiman[7] contends that "progressive politics has allowed its energies to flow into tribal channels of competitive victimhood in which the Enlightenment ideas enshrined in the Universal Declaration of Human Rights have given way to the belief that group identities based on race, gender, sexuality, or ethnicity have the primary claim on allegiance."[8] Social cohesion, cosmopolitanism, and citizenship are undermined by this trend, as it contributes to the more divisive and polarizing politics that are widely acknowledged today.

The struggle against illiberalism continues with recognition that liberal democracy is and must remain the established and preferred form of Western government. This would have been a given in the recent past but requires affirmation today because some critics call for its end. It is difficult to credit their thinking on any level; there is no coherent thought about process and consequences, though we can surmise that the result would be authoritarianism on the left or right without the components of liberal democracy – the rule of law, a market economy, freedom of expression, other rights and freedoms, and institutions of government that protect and advance them.

The struggle continues further through action to protect freedom of expression. Western democracies are resilient, but it is questionable whether they can long withstand the attacks on freedom of expression that we witness today. Episodes recounted in this volume are troubling enough, but a culture of silencing and self-censorship is more so. Repression of freedom of expression comes in the name of combating various wrongs, but there is not a consensus on the nature and extent of these wrongs, and we must insist that people be free to express themselves as long as they don't violate the law. Of course, this does not mean that obnoxious or intemperate speech is tolerable anywhere and anytime. Speech may be regulated in places and at events by those responsible for them, and people may suffer adverse social and professional consequences on account of intemperate or irresponsible remarks.

What is particularly troubling today is the co-option of officialdom into the repression of speech – a cultural phenomenon that reflects the censorious and judgmental era in which we live. Schools, school boards, student leaders, and university officials have been implicated here, driven by their personal views or a like-minded consensus on what can be said, written, or simply available on bookshelves, and some are quick to denounce those against whom they act as hateful, racist, or phobic. These behaviours may not yet be widespread, but they are observable and growing, and we should remind ourselves of history's lessons that repression – and authoritarianism – may begin slowly and spread quickly. The Charter right of freedom of speech must be defended and enforced against those who would diminish it.

The struggle against illiberalism also requires a reassertion of Crick's vision of politics. Recall that Crick thought of politics as a realistic good, a process of discussion and resolution dependent upon virtues that emphasize accommodation, and he worried about influences in its way. Principal among them is ideology, a body of beliefs usually thought of in contrast or conflict with other ideologies.

Competing systems of beliefs do not make for the kind of politics envisaged by Crick; they make for entrenched views and polarization, and when joined with other foes of politics they diminish political culture. One of these foes is populism; it remains a force and possibly a resurgent one if Donald Trump succeeds in his pursuit of a return to the White House in 2024. Another foe is the flight from reason discussed in chapter two as reasoned thought and argument are displaced by feelings, resentments, and moral certitude.

The decline of professional journalism and the rise of social media and artificial intelligence are also threatening to liberalism, and regulation is required to curtail their threat. A regulatory regime is under development. A 2020 report from the Forum for Information and Democracy[9] offered recommendations to thirty-eight countries, including Canada. Recommendations called for mandatory safety and quality requirements, making corrections where a story is determined to be false, and included suggestions to address fact-checking, disclosure of reasons for recommending content to users, micro-targeting, excluding classes of people from content, and banning interfaces intended to make it difficult for users, for example, in deleting their accounts. Canada's Broadcasting and Telecommunications Review Panel joined the call to regulate social media and Bill C-11 passed through Parliament and received Royal assent in the spring of 2023. It is framework legislation primarily aimed at ensuring Canadian and diverse content, though it also expands the potential reach of the Canadian Radio and Television Commission by including online streaming within its mandate. How that authority is exercised remains to be seen.

Artificial intelligence will add to the challenges. Its origins are machines, not people, and its disinformation potential is high. AI systems are emerging at rapid speed, for example, with the release of ChatGPT in 2022 we now have a machine that can respond to questions with human-like answers. "What started out as a panic among educators about ChatGPT's use to cheat on homework assignments has expanded to broader concerns about the ability of the latest crop of 'generative AI' tools to mislead people, spread falsehoods, violate copyright protections and upend some jobs."[10] The European Union has taken the lead in developing a regulatory framework through its proposed Artificial Intelligence Act, which assesses four levels of AI risks to the health, safety, or rights of people: unacceptable, high, limited, and minimal. AI presenting unacceptable risks is banned, and the others are regulated according to their risk levels.[11] If the Act becomes law, it could set a global standard for regulating AI.

Is the decline of professional journalism in the face of social media and AI a harbinger of change or an irreversible trend? Sabrina Wilkinson urges caution here: "fewer journalists are working for organizations and in permanent positions," but "there may have been an increase in journalistic jobs in emerging news organizations, alongside the slew of reported cuts that have taken place at traditional news firms."[12] Of course, the question is not simply about numbers of working journalists; it is also about whether the conditions under which they work afford them opportunities to meet high journalistic standards, and there are different views among journalists about what those standards are. One study reveals two camps: traditionally oriented and engagement oriented.[13] For the traditionalists, restoring trust in journalism "means doubling down on objectivity, transparency and accuracy"[14]; for the engagement oriented, trust depends on relationships – and commitments – seen to be necessary in contemporary journalism. One writer calls it social journalism,[15] and it may be overtaking the traditional model. If it does, what Martin Wolf described as the critical filtering function of professional journalism will be further compromised because that function requires objectivity, transparency, and accuracy.

The media remains topical in our transition to the institutions of democracy and the market economy. Independent media and professional journalism are themselves vital democratic institutions, and protecting their vitality must be part of a liberal agenda. Social media and AI are realities, and they afford wide availability for opportunities to be heard to all voices – extreme and moderate, ignorant and informed. Professional journalism is an assurance of standards that can reduce the potential impact of extremism and ignorance. However, it is dependent upon the trust of readers and listeners, and that trust is declining. Growing numbers of Canadians surveyed by the Edelman Trust Barometer believe that journalists try to mislead, endeavour to support a particular political viewpoint, and are not objective or non-partisan.[16] Public subsidies for professional journalism are not in and of themselves objectionable, but they should be resisted unless it can be shown that recipients are committed to restoring and sustaining trust.

In 2018 the federal government announced measures to support Canadian news media. The idea is not new: "government help for print media has been provided in several countries for decades without compromising editorial independence."[17] The government pledged $600 million in subsidies: a labour tax credit to improve salaries for journalists; allowing not-for-profit news organizations to apply for charitable status; and a tax credit for digital news subscriptions from qualified outlets.[18] Fairness and transparency in determining eligibility are critical here, and it is difficult to persuade Canadians they are present with current levels of mistrust in both.

A Macdonald-Laurier paper published in June 2023 contends that a national news media policy could maintain public trust and ensure a free and independent media.[19] Among its proposals is a call for reform of the CBC, "which is not a pure-play public broadcaster; it is also a commercial competitor – heavily subsidized by public funds – to all other private news organizations, distorting the media landscape and limiting opportunities for competition."[20]

Information literacy must also be improved. The Association of College and Research Libraries describes information literacy as "the ability to find, evaluate, organize, use and communicate information in all its various formats, most notably in situations requiring decision making, problem solving, or the acquisition of knowledge. It is a combination of research skills, critical thinking skills, computer technology skills and communication skills."[21] Information literacy should be a mandatory course of instruction for high school and university students.

Powerful cases have been made for the betterment of Canada's political institutions, and it is getting late to avoid or defer necessary reforms. The Senate has received the most attention over the years, and the focus of change in that body should be on provincial numbers, particularly the differences between the Maritime and Western provinces. British Columbia is 130 times the area of Prince Edward Island, with thirty times the population and six Senate seats compared to the latter's four. Nova Scotia and New Brunswick each have ten Senators compared to six in each of the four larger and more populous western provinces. The historical justification is that Senate representation is by region, not province (though Ontario and Quebec are each counted as a region), but it is provinces that are the principal subdivisions of the country and there are significant differences among them even within their regions. A Triple-E Senate (equal, effective, and elected) appears to be politically unachievable, but a reapportionment of seat numbers should not be. With present membership grandparented in their seats until the mandatory retirement age of seventy-five, new numbers that better reflect the country should be within reach.

Reform of the House of Commons and the offices of party leaders must proceed hand in hand. A stronger role for individual MPs and party caucuses requires that party leaders cede some of their authority over them. With respect to the government, this means the restoration of cabinet as a decision-making body and a caucus with the authority to hold prime ministers to account, as in Great Britain and Australia. Canadian prime ministers' offices have been too powerful in recent years, and officials in them do not have the responsibilities of elected office and are not representative of the country in the way cabinet must be.

We have seen calls for the end of capitalism and market economies noted in the attack on liberalism. Those calling for their end presumably favour state ownership or control – old ideas that have proven oppressive and unworkable – though a need for change in our economy is widely acknowledged. In the aftermath of the Great Recession of 2007–9, Dominic Barton wrote: "the most consequential outcome of the crisis is the challenge to capitalism itself."[22] Most government and business leaders, he said, "share the belief that capitalism has been and can continue to be the greatest engine of prosperity ever devised – and that we will need it to be at the top of its job-creating, wealth-generating game in the years to come."[23] For this to happen, changes are required in the ways corporations are governed, managed, and led.

Precisely what changes are necessary is the important question. Dominic Barton emphasized longer term perspectives, serving stakeholders as well as shareholders and improving the ability of boards to govern like owners.[24] Unpacking where these lead is not a simple exercise, and in general there are two views. One contemplates a focus on stakeholders as distinct from shareholders, an endorsement of stakeholder capitalism. Customers, lenders, suppliers, employees, communities, governments, and society at large are stakeholders, and one report states that company directors should "create and share value among all stakeholders."[25] The second view emphasizes that "a board of

directors' primary duty is to shareholders, the owners who
elect or appoint directors and whose capital is at primary
risk."[26] The second view is the better one. A corporate board
is not a mini-government equipped to weigh and balance
perceived competing interests of stakeholders, all of whom
have a claim on the company's attention and resources. Its
experience, focus, and energy must be on those who put
them on boards and whose investments make it possible for
their companies to do business.

But – and it is an important but – the drive for reform of
capitalism is strong and it must be demonstrated anew that
capitalism serves broader public interests. In particular, it
must be demonstrated that capitalism and improving equality are compatible and that the wealth generated by capitalism can improve well-being across income groups. The
burden for this does not lie on companies and their directors
alone. We have seen in this book that the Canadian economy
is struggling with a particularly serious productivity problem. Experienced voices have called for concerted attention
to a wider economic and policy context; unless and until this
happens, we cannot expect economic performance that can
support greater wealth and its wider distribution.

Business has a central role here, and the two views noted
above are not polar opposites. Excellent directors understand that their companies will not be successful if their
stakeholders are dissatisfied. An emphasis on outstand-
ing governance with measurable indicators, adaptation
to higher expectations in a rapidly changing world, and
responsiveness to those expectations will be required for the
future success of capitalism.

Conclusion

The components of the struggle against illiberalism are now clear. Freedom of expression is under attack, and here we must recall Beverley McLachlin's emphasis on its centrality in free and democratic societies and also as an "indispensable condition of nearly every other freedom."[27] Its attackers are intolerant, officious, and coercive, and a relentless pushback is essential in defence of this freedom.

Polarization is another foe of liberalism, and it is increasing with ideology and populism among its influencers. In Canada, the political parties that contend for federal government are more polarized with Conservatives moving further right and some exploring breakaway options, and Liberals moving further left, adopting an apologetic attitude for the history of the country and less attentive to national unity. The question "can the centre hold?" has been overtaken; it no longer holds, and its restoration requires a re-imagination of politics as understood and explained by Crick. Polarization in Canada has not advanced to the point that its reversal is unlikely or a remote prospect, but it will require leadership and a change in substance and tone.

Effective and trusted institutions are vital in the struggle against illiberalism. The restoration of cabinet government; Senate reform, particularly in representation from each province; a House of Commons in which members are freer to speak their minds without being overseen by the prime minister's office; a revitalized public service; and a strengthened professional and independent media – all are needed and should be achievable if the will is present. Trust is more

difficult to come by: reforms are necessary, though not sufficient for its restoration. Trust comes from confidence in
institutions, information, and people, and indicators tell us
that all three are absent. It will grow only when most Canadians believe that institutions are responsive to their will,
information is reliable and office holders are forthright and
motivated by the best interests of the country. An obstacle
here is the cynicism that is pervasive in public discourse
today; commentators are prepared to attribute motives to
public office holders that they would find deeply troubling
if turned upon themselves. Cynicism is contagious and
destructive to reform and so must be resisted.

The struggle against illiberalism must demonstrate that
liberal democracies afford the best opportunities to their
citizens for successful lives. Their protection of individual
rights and freedoms is superior to others, though this book
records that they are assailable even in liberal jurisdictions
and cannot be taken for granted.

We conclude with the subject of equality. Populations in
failed economic systems or in those that perform poorly
may share equally in outcomes, but their equal shares of
poor outcomes do not afford them the resources they need.
Capitalism is a successful economic system which has provided wide opportunities for participation in the economy,
though its rewards are unevenly distributed. Some of its
critics have claimed that equal opportunity is not available
under capitalism; others say that even if available equal
opportunity is not enough; broadly mandated equal outcomes are necessary to achieve equality. Neither claim is
persuasive. My argument is that equality before and under

the law, and equal opportunity, are the requirements of lib-eralism, though the latter must be attentive to outcomes and must rest upon economic performance, providing wide access to employment and to the middle class.

Race-based initiatives are becoming more common, and how they square with equality and the right to be free from discrimination is an important question. Our starting point is that freedom from racial discrimination is a Charter right and fundamental value, which means that affirmative action under section 15(2) should be interpreted with caution to mean that only minimal intrusion upon the right should be permissible. The paradigm example here is the University of Calgary's cluster hiring initiative. Forty-five academic positions for which white males who are neither LGBTQ2S nor disabled are ineligible to apply is an affront to the rights of disqualified potential candidates to freedom from dis-crimination, and a broad violation of equality. Hopefully one or more of those disqualified will bring the matter to court to obtain judicial clarification on the reach of affirma-tive action.

Afterword: Social Cohesion

Episodes of illiberalism continue to accumulate with our latest example provided by the war between Israel and Hamas. A member of the Ontario Legislature, a Victoria city councillor, a director-level executive at the University of Alberta, and a unionist purporting to represent a chapter of the Alberta Union of Provincial employees were among the scores of Canadians who signed an open letter condemning Israel, denying Hamas atrocities, and designating "so-called Canada" as "a settler colonial and genocidal country, and a supporter of white settler politics in the Middle East and elsewhere as a condition of its own existence." The writers accused Canadian parliamentarians of complicity with genocide and called for their resignations.

Describing this letter as illiberal is an understatement; it is extremist, ahistorical, and disloyal. It cannot be dismissed as simply a difference of opinion. It articulates an unbridgeable divide in which one side ignores known facts and denies the legitimate existence of Canada as well as Israel. It admits of no room for debate and mocks the idea of social cohesion.

Social cohesion is about the ties that bind – in this book, the ties that bind us to Canada as a liberal democratic state. They are found in our connections to one another and in the stories we tell about those connections. These stories may be shared unevenly, but they have to be present as touchstones in our lives by which we gauge who and where we are. We grow up learning them, modify our understandings through time and experience, and develop perspectives on them that we share with others. Stories help us to build social cohesion and citizenship.

Most Canadians grew up with stories about their country that are, on the whole, positive. A half continent of 10 million square kilometres, with Indigenous peoples numbering between a half million and two million[1] evolved over four centuries to become a modern, pluralist democracy with an enviable constitution and standard of living, and unsurpassed protection of rights and freedoms for its population of forty million. Newcomers who have joined us have done so because they see these qualities in their new country. These are not tales of an unblemished past and present – no country can claim them – but they are chronicles about the evolution of a country that has been highly successful by any standard of global comparison.

These stories are being undermined by illiberalism. Ideologies at variance with them have become more common and a dark counter-narrative has emerged: Canada is a racist, genocidal state in which hate and white supremacy are

prominent. This counter-narrative is inaccurate – wildly so –
but its promoters are confirmed in their opinions, disdainful
of those who believe otherwise, and committed to an agenda
that admits of no legitimate dissent. The counter-narrative
may play out in episodes such as the one that leads this
afterword, or in growing numbers of instances in which dissenters are shunned as cruel foes unworthy of civil replies.
An example of the latter is Prime Minister Trudeau's denunciation of New Brunswick Premier Higgs who proposed to
revisit policy that denies parents of students under the age
of sixteen a right to know and give consent to their children identifying as trans by changing their names and pro-
nouns in schools. For Mr. Trudeau, this was an example of
"far right political actors ... trying to outdo themselves with
the types of cruelty and isolation they can inflict on these
already vulnerable people."[2] There is no room for debate
here – even as between the country's first minister and one
of his provincial counterparts – no place for acknowledg-
ing difference of opinion, advancing counter-argument, and
reaching for understanding.

This is the core problem of illiberalism, and it is found
even in places that we might have thought unlikely. At Harvard University, 120 faculty members have come together
"to respond to perceived assaults on free inquiry and a
climate of eroded trust that some faculty and students say
stifles dissent."[3] At universities across America (they might
have added Canada too) there have been "many instances
in which professors have been mobbed, cursed, heckled
into silence and sometimes assaulted ... mirrored by a less

publicly visible silencing of students who, fearing reprisal, are unwilling to discuss certain topics in class."[4] Two of the Harvard faculty, professors Madras and Pinker, describe how such censorship and self-censorship takes hold in academic settings when a small number of committed individuals disrupt events, use social media to engage physical or electronic mobs, and slander their targets "with crippling accusations of racism, sexism or transphobia in a society that rightly abhors them." At the same time, they add, "[a]n expanding bureaucracy for policing harassment and discrimination has professional interests that are not necessarily aligned with the production of knowledge. Department heads, deans and presidents strive to minimize bad publicity and may proffer whatever statement they hope may make the trouble go away."[5]

Social cohesion in Canada is declining, and in a large, decentralized federation in which national unity is already a challenge, the decline is dangerous and could prove fatal. Illiberalism is at the root of this decline. Steven Holmes and before him Fritz Stern remind us that "the features of illiberalism can be understood as a single movement or school of thought."[6] Antiliberals generally "have disdained the liberal habits of tolerance, debate [and] openness."[7] They have momentum and threaten democracy, but the issues are not insurmountable; trends can be reversed, but only if there is leadership to halt and then reverse them. This leadership is missing at the political level, but it can come from the bottom up, and when Anne Applebaum calls for a ferocious fight for liberalism she is not waiting for the fight to be led by political, university or other leaders. She knows it can be won only if moderate voices speak up, are heard, and joined. It must be citizens, rising numbers of them, who confront the illiberal wave and restore liberalism to its rightful place in our public lives.

Endnotes

Foreword

1 Hobbes, *Leviathon Introduction by A.D. Lindsay* (London: J.M. Dent and Sons, 1914) xix.
2 Lindsay, *Introduction*, xix.
3 Lindsay, *Introduction*, xix.
4 Bernard Crick, *In Defence of Politics*, 4th ed. (Chicago: The University of Chicago Press, 1992).
5 Crick, *In Defence of Politics*, 141.
6 Crick, *In Defence of Politics*, 141.
7 Crick, *In Defence of Politics*, 141.
8 Crick, *In Defence of Politics*, 33.
9 Crick, *In Defence of Politics*, 140.
10 Crick, *In Defence of Politics*, 34.
11 Crick, *In Defence of Politics*, 73.
12 Crick, *In Defence of Politics*, 74.
13 Crick, *In Defence of Politics*, 93.
14 Crick, *In Defence of Politics*, 111, 123, 131.
15 Crick, *In Defence of Politics*, 139.
16 Crick, *In Defence of Politics*, 160.
17 Crick, *In Defence of Politics*, 55.

Introduction

1 John Stuart Mill, *On Liberty* (Seattle: Amazon Classics, 2017).
2 Mill, *On Liberty*, 10.

3　Mill, *On Liberty*, 12.

4　Mill, *On Liberty*, 85.

5　Mill, *On Liberty*, 86.

6　Mill, *On Liberty*, 13.

7　Mill, *On Liberty*, 13.

8　Mill, *On Liberty*, 12.

9　Mill, *On Liberty*, 13.

10　See, for example, Gertrude Himmelfarb, *On Liberty and Liberalism: The Case of John Stuart Mill* (New York: Alfred A. Knopf, 1974).

11　Francis Fukuyama, *Liberalism and Its Discontents* (New York: Farrar, Straus and Giroux, 2022).

12　Fukuyama, *Liberalism and It's Discontents*. Jacket.

13　Mark Lilla, *The Once and Future Liberal* (New York, London, Toronto, Sydney: Harper, 2017).

14　Lilla, *The Once and Future Liberal*, 5.

15　Lilla, *The Once and Future Liberal*, 9.

16　Charles Noble, *The Collapse of Liberalism* (Latham, MD: Rowman & Littlefield Publishers, Inc., 2004).

17　Peter MacKinnon, *University Commons Divided* (Toronto, Buffalo, London: University of Toronto Press, 2018).

18　Peter MacKinnon, *Canada in Question* (Toronto, Buffalo, London: University of Toronto Press, 2022).

19　Christopher Dummitt and Zachary Patterson, *The Viewpoint Diversity Crisis at Canadian Universities: Political Homogeneity, Self-Censorship, and Threats to Academic Freedom* (Ottawa: Macdonald-Laurier Institute, 2022).

20　Dummitt and Patterson, *The Viewpoint Diversity Crisis at Canadian Universities*, 4.

21　Dummitt and Patterson, *The Viewpoint Diversity Crisis at Canadian Universities*, 4.

1. In Freedom's Name

1　Joey Chini, "Read the Full Transcript of Emergencies Act Inquiry Commissioner Paul Rouleau's Statement" *CTV News*, 17 February 2023.
　　This protest is to be contrasted with rail blockades in early 2020. CN Rail's Eastern Canada operations and VIA's passenger service across the country were shut down after four hundred trains were cancelled because of Indigenous blockades of rail lines. There were blockades in Ontario, Quebec, and British Columbia, and other transportation routes were closed or compromised, with disruption to the lives and businesses of millions of Canadians. The blockades went on for weeks at costs multiple those of the truckers protest. The Emergencies Act was neither invoked nor apparently contemplated.

2　Christopher Nardi, "Court Rules Use of Emergencies Act Was Unjustified, Unreasonable" *National Post*, 23 January 2024.

3 Roberto Wakerell-Cruz, "Poilievre Says Canada Will Be 'The Freest Country in the World' When He Is Prime Minister" *The Post Millennial*, 14 March 2022.

4 Colin R. Singer, "Canada Ranks Sixth on Freedom Index, Says Fraser Institute Study" *www.immigration.ca*, 2021.

5 Wakerell-Cruz, "Poilievre Says Canada Will Be 'The Freest Country in the World' When He Is Prime Minister."

6 Alan Cairns, John C. Courtney, Peter MacKinnon, Hans J. Michelmann and David Smith, eds., *Citizenship, Diversity and Pluralism* (Montreal, Kingston: McGill-Queen's University Press, 1999) 11.

7 Cairns et al., *Citizenship, Diversity and Pluralism*, 11.

8 Cairns et al., *Citizenship, Diversity and Pluralism*, 11.

9 Trent University Freedom Lounge, www.reddit.com.

10 Trent University Freedom Lounge, www.reddit.com.

11 Trent University Freedom Lounge, www.Reddit.com.

12 As president of the University of Saskatchewan, I had two opportunities to consider space designated exclusively for a racial or religious group. The Gordon Oakes Red Bear Student Centre was among my initiatives to attract and retain Indigenous students. My advisor on all matters Indigenous was George Lafond of the Muskeg Lake Cree Nation and former Chief of the Saskatoon Tribal Council. The question arose: would this space be for Indigenous students alone, or would it be for Indigenous and non-Indigenous students to come together to learn from and better understand one another? Mr. Lafond and I insisted upon the latter, a choice symbolized in the name by joining the Indigenous and anglicized names of its namesake.

   On the second occasion I was asked by the Muslim Students Association to identify space where Muslim students could pray. I replied that I was confident that the university could accommodate their request, but I was then informed that the space had to be theirs alone to accommodate their five daily prayers and the protocols associated with them. This request I declined, informing them that as a public, secular institution the University of Saskatchewan would not designate space exclusively for any single religious group.

13 Alex Anas Ahmed, "Ontario Schools Hold Book-Burning Ceremony for 'Reconciliation'" *The Post Millennial*, 8 September 2021.

14 "College Student Views on Free Expression and Campus Speech 2022" *Knight Foundation*, 25 January 2022.

15 "College Student Views on Free Expression and Camus Speech 2022" *Knight Foundation*, 25 January 2022.

16 "2022 Free Speech Rankings" *Foundation for Individual Rights and Expression*, rankings.thefire.org.

17 "2022 Free Speech Rankings."

18 Frederick M. Hess and Grant Addison, "College Leaders Think Free Speech Is at Risk Everywhere – Except on Their Own Campuses" 14 February 2018, www.aei.org.

19 "The 'Banned' List. Academics for Academic Freedom" 2022, www.afaf
    .org.uk.
20 "Higher Education: Free Speech and Academic Freedom" *Policy Paper*,
    2021, www.gov.uk.
21 "Free Speech in Universities: New Data Reveals Student and Public
    Perceptions" *King's College London News Centre*, 29 September 2022.
22 "Free Speech in Universities: New Data Reveals Student and Public
    Perceptions."
23 "Free Speech in Universities: New Data Reveals Student and Public
    Perceptions."
24 "French Review Finds No Campus Free Speech Crisis" *Universities
    Australia*, 8 April 2019, www.universitiesaustralia.edu.AU.
25 David Farrar, "Ranking the Universities on Free Speech" *New Zealand
    Free Speech Union*, 2022, www.kiwiblog.co.nz.
26 Lilla, *The Once and Future Liberal*, 6.
27 Lilla, *The Once and Future Liberal*, 6, 7.
28 Lilla, *The Once and Future Liberal*, 7.
29 Lilla, *The Once and Future Liberal*, 10.
30 Lilla, *The Once and Future Liberal*, 64, 65.
31 Fukuyama, *Liberalism and Its Discontents*, 97.
32 Fukuyama, *Liberalism and Its Discontents*, 97.
33 Fukuyama, *Liberalism and Its Discontents*, jacket.
34 Noble, *The Collapse of Liberalism*, 163.
35 Noble, *The Collapse of Liberalism*, 163.
36 Jeffrey Simpson, "The Liberals' Downward Slide" *The Globe and Mail*, 29
    October 2022, 8.
37 Simpson, "The Liberals' Downward Slide" 8.
38 Simpson, "The Liberals' Downward Slide" 9.
39 Simpson, "The Liberals' Downward Slide" 9.
40 Simpson, "The Liberals' Downward Slide" 9.
41 Simpson, "The Liberals' Downward Slide" 9.
42 [2001] 1 SCR 45, at para. 23 (SCC).
43 Kent Roach and David Schneiderman, "Freedom of Expression in
    Canada" (2013), 61 *SCLR (2d)*, 429.
44 Tyler Dawson, "Excusive: Wilfrid Laurier University Asks Court to
    Dismiss Jordan Peterson Lawsuit" *National Post*, 8 December 2022.

2. The Decline of Politics

1 Foreword.
2 Anne Applebaum, "There Is No Liberal World Order" *The Atlantic*, 31
   March 2022.
3 Colin Robertson, "Liberal Internationalism for the 21st Century" 21
   October 2016, *colinrobertson.ca*.
4 David Johnston, *Trust: Twenty Ways to Build a Better Country* (Toronto:
   McClelland & Stewart, 2018), 4.

5 Applebaum, "There Is No Liberal World Order."
6 Applebaum, "There Is No Liberal World Order."
7 Applebaum, "There Is No Liberal World Order."
8 Crick, *In Defence of Politics*, 34.
9 Crick, *In Defence of Politics*, 34.
10 Maurice Cranston, "Ideology" *Britannica*, 1999.
11 Hannah Arendt, *The Origins of Totalitarianism* (New York: Schocken Books, 1951).
12 See, for example, Nathan Vanderklippe, "In Texas, Members of LGTBQ Community Arm Themselves to Fight Right-Wing Extremists" *The Globe and Mail*, 27 November 2022.
13 Steven Levitsky and Daniel Ziblatt, *How Democracies Die* (New York: Broadway Books, 2018), 9.
14 The *New York Times*'s Roger Cohen writes: "populists may be authoritarians, ethnonationalists, nativists, leftists, rightists, xenophobes, proto-fascists, fascists, autocrats, losers from globalization, moneyed provocateurs, conservatives, socialists, and just plain and unhappy or frustrated or bored people – anyone, from the crazed to the rational, from the racist to the tolerant, energized by social media to declare the liberal democratic rules-based consensus that has broadly prevailed since the end of the Cold War is not for them" (Roger Cohen, "It's Time to Depopularize 'Populist'" *New York Times*, 13 July 2018, www.nytimes.com).
15 Cas Mudde and Crostobal Rovira Laltwasser, "Voices of the Peoples: Populism in Europe and Latin America Compared," *Kellogg Institute Working Paper no. 378*, 2011.
16 Mudde and Rovira Laltwasser, "Voices of the Peoples."
17 Mudde and Rovira Laltwasser, "Voices of the Peoples."
18 Mudde and Rovira Laltwasser, "Voices of the Peoples," 9, where the authors credit Freeden (1996) and Laclau (1977), Lane Crothers, "Populism," *Brill Masthead*, brill.com.
19 Norm Gidron and Bart Bonikowski, "Varieties of Populism: Literature Review and Research Agenda" *Working Paper Series*, Weatherhead Center for International Affairs, Harvard University, no. 13-0004 (2013) 6, https://ssrn.com/abstract=2459387.
20 Gidron and Bonikowski, "Varieties of Populism," 7.
21 Gidron and Bonikowski, "Varieties of Populism," 10.
22 Andre Munro, "Populism: Political Program or Movement" *Encyclopedia Britannica*, https//www.britannica.com.
23 Elena Block and Ralph Negrine, "The Populist Communication Style: Toward a Critical Framework" *International Journal of Communication* 11 (2017): 178–97, https://core.ac. See also page 9, where the authors credit Freeden (1996) and Laclau.
24 Block and Negrine, "The Populist Communication Style," 181.
25 Block and Negrine, "The Populist Communication Style," 182.
26 Michael Hatherall, "Populist Narratives and the Making of National Strategy" *The Bridge* (2018).

27 Hatherall, "Populist Narratives."
28 Hatherall, "Populist Narratives."
29 Claes H. de Vreese, Frank Esser, Toril Aalberg, Carsten Reinemann, and James Stanyer, "Populism as an Expression of Political Communication Content and Style: A New Perspective" *International Journal of Press/Politics* 23, no. 4 (2018): 423–38, at 28; Cas Mudde, "Populism in the Twenty-First Century: An Illiberal Democratic Response to Undemocratic Liberalism" *Penn Arts and Sciences*, University of Pennsylvania, 2020, www.sas.UPenn.edu.
30 de Vreese et al., "Populism as an Expression" 424n23.
31 de Vreese et al., "Populism as an Expression" 424n23.
32 Clive Cook, "Populists Aren't the Only Enemies of Liberal Democracy" *Bloomberg Opinion*, 1 August 2018, www.bloomberg.com.
33 Moises Naim, "How to Be a Populist" *The Atlantic*, 21 April 2017, www.theatlantic.com.
34 Fred Wertheimer, "Trump's Big Lie Continues to Damage Our Democracy," 11 August, 2022, organyzepro.com.
35 Zoe Richards, "Republican Kari Lake Files Lawsuit in Bid to Overturn Arizona Election" *NBC News*, 10 December 2022, www.cnbc.com.
36 Kristen Holmes, "Trump Calls for the Termination of the Constitution in Truth Social Post" *CNNpolitics*, 4 December 2022, www.cnn.com.
37 C.J. Werleman, "Millions of Pro-Trump Americans Support Political Violence" *Byline Times*, 12 January 2022, bylinetimes.com.
38 Cite 6 January committee report.
39 Donald Trump quoted in Siba Jackson, "January 6 Committee Recommends Criminal Charges Against Donald Trump" *Sky News*, 19 December 2022, Sky UK Limited.
40 Jude Sheerin and Rebecca Seales, "What's in the Trump Indictment: U.S. Nuclear Secrets and Files Kept in Shower" *BBC News*, Washington, DC, 9 June 2023, www.bbc.com.
41 Tom Slater, "Populism Is Bigger than Trump" *Spiked*, 16 November 2022, www.spiked-online.com.
42 "Populists in Power Around the World" *Tony Blair Institute for Global Change* (2018), www.institute.global/policy.
43 Jack Dickens, "The New World: The Populist Revolution Is Here to Stay" *Reaction*, 24 August 2020, reaction.life.
44 David Laycock writes that populism "has a long history in Canada and continues to be an important factor in Canadian political culture and public life. There have been right wing populist parties (e.g. Social Credit Party, Creditistes, Reform) and left-wing populist parties (e.g. United Farmers of Alberta, Co-operative Commonwealth Federation)" (David Laycock, "Populism in Canada" *The Canadian Encyclopedia*, 2006, www.theCanadianencyclopedia.ca).
45 Dale Eisler and Kevin Lynch, "The Truckers Convoy: Examining the Consequences for Canada" *Johnson-Shoyama Graduate School of Public Policy*, 9 March 2022, www.schoolofpublicpolicy.sk.ca.

46 Eisler and Lynch, "The Truckers Convoy."
47 Steven Pinker, *Enlightenment Now: The Case for Reason, Science, Humanism and Progress* (New York: Viking, 2018) 8.
48 Pinker, *Enlightenment Now*, 8, 9.
49 Pinker, *Enlightenment Now*, 5.
50 Pinker, *Enlightenment Now*, 6.
51 Pinker, *Enlightenment Now*, 365.
52 Pinker, *Enlightenment Now*, 365.
53 Pinker, *Enlightenment Now*, 5.
54 Pinker, *Enlightenment Now*, book jacket.
55 Albert Salomon, "In Praise of the Enlightenment: In Commemoration of Fontenelle, 1657–1757," *Social Research* 24, no. 2 (Summer 1957), www.jstor.org.
56 Anthony Pagden, *The Enlightenment and Why It Still Matters* (New York: Penguin Random House, 2013), (Kirkus Reviews), www.penguinrandomhouse.com.
57 A.C. Grayling, "How to Defend the Enlightenment: A Full Transcript of the Discussion between Anthony Grayling and Tvetan Todorov," *New Humanist*, 15 January 2010. new humanist.org.Ukraine.
58 Phil Badger, "What's Wrong with the Enlightenment?" *Philosophy Now*, 2010, philosophynow.org.
59 Stephen Eric Bonner, "Interpreting the Enlightenment: Metaphysics, Critique, and Politics," *Logos Journal*, 2004, logosjournal.com.
60 Bonner, "Interpreting the Enlightenment."
61 Introduction, n. 20.
62 Chapter one, n. 34.
63 Eisler and Lynch, "The Truckers Convoy."
64 Levitsky and Ziblatt, "How Democracies Die."

3. Confronting Hate

1 The Report of the Special Committee on Hate Propaganda in Canada. Queen's Printer and Controller of Stationery, Ottawa. p. 327.
2 Gunther Plaut, *Book Review: The Report of the Special Committee on Hate Propaganda in Canada* (York University: Osgoode Hall Law Journal, volume 5, number 2, 1967, 313–17), 315.
3 Kundera Provost-Yombo, Cynthia Louden, and Susan McDonald, "Hate as an Aggravating Factor at Sentencing: A Review of the Case Law from 2007–2020" Department of Justice Canada, 2020, www.justice.gc.ca.
4 Criminal Code (Canada), section 319.
5 *R. v. Keegstra* [1990] 3 S.C.R. 697.
6 Keegstra.
7 Statistics Canada reported that police-reported hate crimes experienced a 27 per cent increase in 2021 over 2020; a 30 per cent increase in 2020, and a 72 per cent increase from 2019 to 2021. Major increases were also reported in the United States and in Europe. See "Police-Reported

Hate Crimes Rise Again as Pandemic Worsens Discrimination: Stats
Can" *CTV News*, 23 March 2023, www.CTVnews.ca; The United States
Department of Justice Updated 2021 Hate Crime Statistics, www.justice
.gov; "Hate Crime, England and Wales, 2021–2022" *Official Statistics*, 6
October 2022, www.gov.uk.

8   Plaut, *Book Review.*
9   Michael Higgins, "Truth Ignored as Teacher Fired for Saying TB Caused
    Residential School Deaths" *National Post*, 21 February 2023, nationalpost.
    com.
10 Olivia Stefanovich, "NDP MP Calls for Hate Speech Law to Combat
    Residential School Denialism" *CBC News*, 18 February 2023,
    www.cbc.ca.
11 Jessica Triff, "Trans Rights? Yes. Toxic In-Your-Face Activism? No" *CBC
    Opinion*, 23 October 2021, www.cbc.ca.
12 Sue-Ann Levy, "Another Ontario Teacher Cancelled for Pushing Back
    against Critical Race Theory" *True North North*, 12 June 2022, tnc.news.
13 Levy, "Another Ontario Teacher."
14 A Letter on Justice and Open Debate, *Harper's Magazine*, 7 July 2020,
    harpers.org.
15 A Letter on Justice and Open Debate.
16 A Letter on Justice ad Open Debate.
17 Harvard's Steven Pinker welcomes new models for universities. He
    writes: "current universities are locked into a strange business model:
    exorbitant tuition, a mushrooming bureaucracy, and obscure admissions
    policies that are neither meritocratic nor egalitarian, combined with
    plummeting intellectual diversity and tolerance for open enquiry."
    See Anemona Hartocollis, "They Say Colleges Are Censorious. So They
    Are Starting a New One" *The New York Times*, 8 November 2021, www
    .newyorktimes.com.
18 Endnote 7.
19 Endnote 7.
20 "Ultra-Nationalism, Anti-Semitism, Anti-Muslim Hatred: Anti-Racism
    Commission Raises Alarm Over Situation in Europe" *Council of Europe*,
    27 February 2020, www.coe.int.
21 "Rwanda Genocide: 100 Days of Slaughter," 4 April 2019, www.bbc
    .com, and "In Kenya, It Is Tribal Violence That Often Underpins Violent
    Extremism" *Institute for Strategic Dialogue*, www.isdglobal.org.
22 "'We Never Came Here by Our Choice' – The Heartache of Religious
    Persecution" *Deseret News*, 7 December 2022, www.deseret.com.
23 Spoken by Juliet, Act 2, Scene 2 in William Shakespeare, *Romeo and Juliet.*

4. The Challenge of Inequality

1   Crick, *In Defence of Politics*, 140. See also chapter 1, n. 9.
2   C.B. Macpherson, *The Life and Times of Liberal Democracy* (Oxford,
    London, New York: Oxford University Press, 1977).

3　Macpherson, *Life and Times*, 1.
4　Macpherson, *Life and Times*, 1.
5　Macpherson, *Life and Times*, 94.
6　Macpherson, *Life and Times*, 97.
7　Macpherson, *Life and Times*, 100.
8　Macpherson, *Life and Times*, 107.
9　Noble, chapter 1, n. 16.
10　Noble, *Collapse of Liberalism*, 1.
11　Noble, *Collapse of Liberalism*, 1.
12　Noble, *Collapse of Liberalism*, 2.
13　Noble, *Collapse of Liberalism*, 2,
14　Noble, *Collapse of Liberalism*, 90.
15　Noble, *Collapse of Liberalism*, 90.
16　Noble, *Collapse of Liberalism*, 91.
17　Noble, *Collapse of Liberalism*, 91.
18　Noble, *Collapse of Liberalism*, 141.
19　Noble, *Collapse of Liberalism*, 118.
20　Noble, *Collapse of Liberalism*, 124, 125.
21　Noble, *Collapse of Liberalism*, 153.
22　Noble, *Collapse of Liberalism*, 157.
23　Joseph E. Stiglitz, *The Price of Inequality: How Today's Divided Society Endangers Our Future* (New York, London: W.W. Norton & Company, 2012), 7.
24　John Peters, *Jobs with Inequality: Financialization, Post-Democracy, and Labour Deregulation in Canada* (Toronto, Buffalo, London: University of Toronto Press, 2022), 3.
25　William Watson, *The Inequality Trap: Fighting Capitalism Instead of Poverty* (Toronto, Buffalo, London: University of Toronto Press, 2015).
26　William Watson, "The Inequality Trap" *National Post*, 30 November 2015, nationalpost.com.
27　Watson, "The Inequality Trap."
28　Quoted by Pierre Desrochers and Joanna Szurmak, *Population Bombed! Exploding the Link between Overpopulation and Climate Change* (London: Global Warming Policy Foundation, 2018), 57.
29　Sarah Burkinshaw, Yaz Terajima, and Carolyn A. Wilkins, "Income Inequality in Canada" *Bank of Canada Staff Discussion Paper*, 2022, 3, www.bankofcanada.ca.
30　Burkinshaw, Terajima and Wilkins, "Income Inequality in Canada."
31　Sharon Miki Chan, "Centi-Millionaire Status: Canada Ranks Eighth in the World for Mega-Rich People," www.slice.ca.
32　Ronald Dworkin discussing his book *Justice for Hedgehogs* in an interview with Joanne Myers. Carnegie Council for Ethics in International Affairs, 2011, www.rimaregas.com.
33　Ronald Dworkin discussing *Justice for Hedgehogs*.
34　Ronald Dworkin discussing *Justice for Hedgehogs*.
35　Ronald Dworkin discussing *Justice for Hedgehogs*.

36   Ronald Dworkin discussing *Justice for Hedgehogs*.
37   Ronald Dworkin discussing *Justice for Hedgehogs*.
38   See, for example, Douglas Bamford's Tax Appeal, 2015, dougstaxappeal. blogspot.com; and Michael Green, Dworkin's Insurance Markets, "Freedom, Markets and Well-Being," 2008, Carneades.pamona.edu.
39   Will Kenton, "What Is Social Capital? Definition, Types and Examples" *Investopedia*, 27 November 2022, www.investopedia.com.
40   Robert D. Putnam, "Better Together: Restoring the American Community" Weatherford Centre for International Affairs at Harvard University, 2004, copy at https://wcfia.harvard.edu/sites/projects .iq.harvard.edu/files/wcfia/files/762_bettertogether.pdf.
41   Hugh Segal and Carolyn Hughes Tuohy, "Equal Opportunity a Right That Canada Must Preserve" *The Globe and Mail*, 18 April 2014, www .theglobeandmail.com.
42   Segal and Tuohy, "Equal Opportunity."
43   Segal and Tuohy, "Equal Opportunity."
44   Segal and Tuohy, "Equal Opportunity."
45   Don Drummond, "Canada's Foggy Economic and Fiscal Future" *C.D. Howe Institute E-Brief*, 20 October 2020, www.cdhowe.org.
46   Paul Wells writes about Morneau's forthcoming book in "Morneau on Trudeau: 'Sorely Lacking'," 6 January 2023, paulwells.sub stack.com.
47   Peter MacKinnon, *Canada in Question: Exploring Our Citizenship in the Twenty-First Century* (Toronto, Buffalo, London: University of Toronto Press, 2022), chapter 5.
48   [[1997] 3 SCR 624.
49   See *Pridgen v. University of Calgary* (2012) ABCA 78 and *R. v. Whatcott* (2012) ABQB 231, two cases in which the University of Calgary sought, unsuccessfully, to prevent Charter scrutiny of university decisions.
50   "Equity, Diversity and Inclusion" (University of Toronto: Division of the Vice-President, Research and Innovation, undated), research.utoronto.ca.
51   Sophia Moreau, *Faces of Inequality: A Theory of Wrongful Discrimination* (New York: Oxford University Press, 2020).
52   Moreau, *Faces of Inequality*, 14, 15.
53   Moreau, *Faces of Inequality*, 219.
54   Moreau, *Faces of Inequality*, 220.
55   Moreau, *Faces of Inequality*, 220.
56   Moreau, *Faces of Inequality*, 220.
57   Moreau, *Faces of Inequality*, 84.
58   Dworkin, chapter 3, n. 35.
59   Moreau, *Faces of Inequality*, 118.
60   *Students for Fair Admission, Inc., Petitioner v. President and Fellows of Harvard College; Students for Fair Admission, Inc., Petitioner v. University of North Carolina et al.*, United States Supreme Court, 29 June 2023.
61   163 U.S. 537 (1896). Fourteenth Amendment, Britannica: https://www .britannica.com/topic/Fourteenth-Amendment.
62   347 U.S. 483 (1954).

63 *Yick Wo v. Hopkins*, 118 U.S. 356 at 369.
64 Students for Fair Admission, n. 60, at 15.
65 *Regents of University of California v. Bakke*, 438 U.S. 265 (1978).
66 Students for Fair Admission, n. 60, at 17.
67 Students for Fair Admission, n. 60, at 18.
68 *Regents of University of California v. Bakke*, n. 65, at 289, 290.
69 Students for Fair Admission, n. 60, at 18.
70 Students for Fair Admission, n. 60, at 18.
71 Students for Fair Admission, n. 60, at 22.
72 Students for Fair Admission, n. 60, at 24.
73 Students for Fair Admission, n. 60, at 26.
74 Students for Fair Admission, n. 60, at 39.
75 Students for Fair Admission, n. 60, at 39.
76 Students for Fair Admission, n. 60, at 26.
77 Moreau, *Faces of Inequality*, n. 60.
78 Applebaum, "There Is No World Liberal Order," chapter 2, n. 7.
79 Christy Somos, "1 in 5 Children Live in Poverty, National Report Card
    Says" 14 January 2020, ctvnews.ca.
80 MacKinnon, *Canada in Question*, chapter 3, n. 48.
81 Dworkin, chapter 3, n. 35.

5. Expectations of Democracy: Institutions, Trust, and Accountability

 1 Adrian Humphreys, "Most Canadians Agree 'Canada Is Broken' – and
    They're Angry About It: National Poll," *National Post*, 4 February 2023, A6.
 2 Peter C. Newman, *The Distemper of Our Times* (Montreal, Kingston:
    McGill-Queen's University Press, 1978).
 3 Janet Ajzenstat, *The Canadian Founding: John Locke and Parliament*
    (Montreal, Kingston: McGill-Queen's University Press, 2007) 181.
 4 Ajzenstat, *The Canadian Founding*, 180.
 5 In March 2021, Prime Minister Trudeau described the Canadian
    Parliament as founded upon "colonialism, or discrimination or systemic
    racism." 9 March 2021, *postmillennial.com*.
 6 Ajzenstat, *The Canadian Founding*, 6.
 7 Ajzenstat, *The Canadian Founding*, 6.
 8 Ajzenstat, *The Canadian Founding*, 47.
 9 David E. Smith, *The Constitution in a Hall of Mirrors: Canada at 150*
    (Toronto, Buffalo, London: University of Toronto Press, 2017) ix.
10 Ajzenstat, *The Canadian Founding*, 20.
11 Donald J. Savoie, *Democracy in Canada: The Disintegration of Our
    Institutions* (Montreal, Kingston: McGill-Queen's University Press, 2019).
12 Savoie, *Democracy in Canada*, 368.
13 Savoie, *Democracy in Canada*, 67.
14 Jonathan Manthorpe, "Canada Has a Serious Democratic Deficit" *The
    Globe and Mail*, 28 August 2020, www.theglobeandmail.com.
15 Manthorpe, "Canada Has a Serious Democratic Deficit."

16 Savoie, *Democracy in Canada*, 187.
17 Savoie, *Democracy in Canada*, 189.
18 Savoie, *Democracy in Canada*, 68.
19 Savoie, *Democracy in Canada*, x.
20 Savoie, *Democracy in Canada*, 237, 238.
21 Savoie, *Democracy in Canada*, 201.
22 Savoie, *Democracy in Canada*, 264n1.
23 Savoie, *Democracy in Canada*, 368.
24 Hayatullah Amanat, "Fewer than One-in-Five Canadians Want
    Monarchy to Continue: Poll" *CTV News*, 16 March 2023, ctvnews.ca.
25 David E. Smith, Christopher McCreery and Jonathan Shanks, *Canada's
    Deep Crown* (Toronto, Buffalo, London: University of Toronto Press,
    2022).
26 Smith et al., *Canada's Deep Crown*, 4.
27 Smith et al., *Canada's Deep Crown*, 29, 30.
28 Smith et al., *Canada's Deep Crown*, 19.
29 Smith et al., *Canada's Deep Crown*, 18, 19.
30 Smith et al., *Canada's Deep Crown*, 36.
31 Smith et al., *Canada's Deep Crown*, 25.
32 David Johnston, *Trust: Twenty Ways to Build a Better Country*
    (Toronto: Penguin Random House, 2018) 1, 2.
33 2023 Edelman Trust Barometer: Navigating a Polarized World,
    www.edelman.com.
34 The Proof Strategies CanTrust Index, 2023, 5. Getronics.com.
35 Johnston, *Trust*, 207. The difference is illustrated in a story from Canada
    Day, 2020. A Halifax daily – the *Chronicle Herald* – apologized for the
    Canadian flag while newly sworn-in Canadians talked about their new
    country. "I started feeling like I belonged to this country," said one new
    Canadian. Another reported amazement at the country's inclusiveness.
    A third was living his "dream of belonging to the Canadian family." Still
    another announced his delight to be a Canadian citizen. Perhaps, on the
    eve of Canada Day, the apologists at the *Chronicle Herald* should have
    hearkened to the voices of our newest Canadians rather than expressing
    their apologies for their country. See "Have a Happy Canada Say. Sorry"
    The Globe and Mail, 1 July 2020, A12; and "I Have Found My Place Here:
    New Canadians Reflect and Offer Advice for Those Just Starting the
    Journey" *The Globe and Mail*, 1 July 2020, A1, A10, A11.
36 "Electoral System and Possible Foreign Interference" *Leger*, 16 March
    2023, leger.360.com.
37 Johnston, *Trust*, 153.
38 Emerald Bensadoun, "Morning Update: Inside Canada's Broken
    Freedom-of Information System: 'An Affront to Democracy'" *The Globe
    and Mail Morning Update Newsletter*, 9 June 2023, www.theglobeandmail
    .com.
39 Bensadoun, "Morning Update."
40 Bensadoun, "Morning Update."

41 David Walmsley, "The Globe's Secret Canada Project Aims to Make
    Governments More Transparent" 9 June 2023, www.theglobeandmail.com.

42 COVID resulted in a decline in sitting days in 2020 but did not begin
    the decline. "Since the beginning of the 1990s … the House has met less
    often. The House sat for an average of just 74 days between January and
    July in the 1990s, dropping to 72 days in the 2000s, and 69 days in the
    2010s – the lowest attendance rate since the days of John A. Macdonald"
    (Eric Grenier, "The House of Commons Just Had One of Its Slowest
    Years in a Century, Thanks to the Pandemic" *CBC News*, 28 June 2020,
    www.cbc.ca).

43 Sabrina Nanji and Bruce Campion-Smith, "Question Period Is Supposed
    to Be about Holding the Government to Account. So How Did It Become
    Political Theatre?" *Toronto Star*, 20 June 2018, www.thestar.com.

44 "Influence of Interest Groups on Policy-Making" *U4 Anti-Corruption
    Resource Centre*, www.transparency.org.

45 Testifying before the House of Commons Standing Committee on Access
    to Information, Privacy and Ethics in May 2021, the commissioner
    stated that there were 6,435 active federal lobbyists in March 2021, the
    highest number ever. See Awanish Sinha, Adam Goldenberg, Amanda
    Larusso, and Aman Gill, "Lobbying Commissioner Recommends
    Significant Changes to Canada's Federal Lobbyist Registration Rules"
    mccarthytetrault, 28 June 2021, www.mccarthy.ca.

46 Lobbying Act (R.S.C., 1985, c.44(4th supp.)) s.14(1).

47 According to the Office of the Commissioner, the Lobbying Act is
    based on four key principles: free and open access to government is
    an important matter of public interest; lobbying public office holders
    is a legitimate activity; it is desirable that public office holders and the
    general public be able to know who is engaged in lobbying activities;
    and the system of registration of paid lobbyists should not impede free
    and open access to government. Office of the Commissioner of Lobbying
    of Canada, 2008, www.lobbycanada.go.ca.

48 Peter Swain quoted in Marci McDonald, "Canada's Star News Anchors,"
    The Canadian Encyclopedia, 17 March 2015.

49 Peter Swain quoted in Marci McDonald, "Canada's Star News Anchors."

50 Peter Swain quoted in Marci McDonald, "Canada's Star News Anchors."

51 Rachel Pulfer, "With the Rise of AI-generated Propaganda, Journalism Is
    More Important Than Ever" *The Globe and Mail*, 3 May 2023.

52 Quoted by Rachel Pulfer, n. 49.

53 Jonathan Haidt, "Why the Last 10 Years of American Life Have Been
    Uniquely Stupid" *The Atlantic*, 11 April 2022, www.theatlantic.com.

54 Haidt, "Why the Last 10 Years of American Life Have Been Uniquely
    Stupid."

55 Haidt, "Why the Last 10 Years of American Life Have Been Uniquely
    Stupid."

56 Haidt, "Why the Last 10 Years of American Life Have Been Uniquely
    Stupid."

6. Overview and Conclusion

1   Tristin Hopper, "Public Health Agency of Canada Report Calls for
    Toppling of 'Capitalism and Liberty'" *National Post*, 20 April 2023,
    nationalpost.com. The seventy-two-page report is titled "What We
    Heard: Perspectives on Climate Change and Public Health in Canada"
    Government of Canada, 17 April 2023, www.canada.ca. The report was
    commissioned by the chief public health officer of Canada.
2   Ajenstat, *The Canadian Founding*, 181, chapter 5, n. 3.
3   See, for example, Aaron Mills, "Rooted Constitutionalism: Growing
    Political Community" in *Resurgence and Reconciliation: Indigenous-Settler
    Relations and Earth Teachings*, edited by Michael Asch, John Borrows
    and James Tully (Toronto: University of Toronto Press, 2018); and
    Glen Coulthard, *Red Skin, White Masks: Rejecting the Colonial Politics of
    Recognition* (Minneapolis: University of Minnesota Press, 2014).
4   Martin Wolf, *The Crisis of Democratic Capitalism* (Penguin Random
    House, 2023) reviewed by Colin Robertson in Policy: Canadian Politics
    and Public Policy, 17 April 2023, www.policymagazine.ca. The quote is
    from Robertson's review.
5   Robertson, *Book Review*.
6   Thor Benson, "This Disinformation Is Just for You" *Security*, 1 August
    2023, www.wired.com/story.
7   Susan Neiman, *Left Is Not Woke* (Cambridge: Polity Press, 2023).
8   As summarized by Fintan O'Toll in "Defying Tribalism," *New York
    Review of Books*, 2 November 2023.
9   "Forum on Information and Democracy 250 Recommendations on How
    to Stop 'Infodemics'" *Reporters Without Borders*, 2020, rsf.org.
10 Matt O'Brien, "ChatGPT Chief Says Artificial Intelligence Should Be
    Regulated by a US or Global Agency" *Toronto Star*, 16 May 2023, www
    .thestar.com.
11 "EU AI Act: First Regulation on Artificial Intelligence" *European
    Parliament News*, 14 June 2023, www.europarl.europa.eu.
12 Sabrina Wilkinson, "Canadian Journalism in Decline: Fewer Permanent
    Jobs, Less Security" *The Conversation*, 19 November 2019, www.
    theconversation.com. See also Sabrina Wilkinson and Dwayne Winseck,
    "Crisis or Transformation? Debates Over Journalistic Work in Canada"
    Canadian Journal of Communication 44, no. 3 (September 2019), cjc.
    utpjournals.press.
13 Mark Coddington and Seth Lewis, "Journalism Face a Crisis in Trust.
    Journalists Fall into Two Very Different Camps for How to Fix It"
    NiemanLab, 8 October 2020, www.niemanlab.org.
14 Coddington and Lewis, "Journalism Faces a Crisis in Trust."
15 Carrie Brown, "Engaged Journalism: It's Finally Happening," *NiemanLab
    Predictions for Journalism*, 2020, www.niemanlab.org.
16 2023 Edelman Trust Barometer, www.Edelman.ca. See also Salmaan
    Farooqui, "People Increasingly Distrust Media, Avoid News Out

of Fatigue, Report Finds" *The Globe and Mail*, 15 June 2022, www .theglobeandmail.com.

17 Bernard Descoteaux and Colette Brin, "Funding for Canadian Media: The Who, Why and How" *Policy Options*, 19 December 2018, policyoptions.ripped.org.

18 Bernard Descoteaux and Colette Brin, Funding for Canadian Media. See also Stuart Thompson, "$600 Million in Federal Funding for Media 'A Turning Point for the Plight of Newspapers in Canada'" *National Post*, 28 November 2018, nationalpost.com.

19 Peter Menzies and Konrad von Finckenstein, "…And Now, the News. A National News Media Policy for Canada" *Macdonald-Laurier Institute*, June 2023, macdonaldlaurier.ca.

20 Reform of the CBC is only one of six elements in the Menzies–von Finckenstein paper. The others are support subscribers through tax benefits; support the digital transformation; change the tax status of current tax benefits/funds; re-evaluate the role of the CRTC; and support the Canadian Journalists Fund.

21 "What Is Information Literacy?" *NAU Cline Library*, nau.edu.

22 Dominic Barton, "Capitalism for the Long Term" *Harvard Business Review*, March 2011, reprinted by McKinsey & Company, www .mckinsey.com.

23 Barton, "Capitalism for the Long Term."

24 Barton, "Capitalism for the Long Term."

25 Brian Gallant, "Navigator Launches the Canadian Centre for the Purpose of the Corporation" *Navigator*, 8 July 2020, navltd.com.

26 Letter to the Institute of Corporate Directors from Art Korpach and Jim Dinning 24 April 2023.

27 [2001] SCR 45 at para 23. (SCC).

Afterword: Social Cohesion

1 "With regards to the population of Aboriginal people in what would become Canada at the beginning of sustained European contact in the early 16 century, estimates vary. Anthropologists and historians have, however, given a tentative range between 350,000 and 500,000 people, with some estimates as high as 2,000,000" (Frank Trovato and Laura Aylsworth, "Demography of Indigenous Peoples in Canada," *The Canadian Encyclopedia*, 1 February 2012, www.theCanadianencyclopedia.ca).

2 Adam Huras, "'We Have to Stand Against This': Trudeau Denounces N.B. Gender Policy" *National Post*, 9 June 2023, nationalpost.com.

3 Jonathan Shaw, "Is Harvard Campus Conversation Constrained?" *Harvard Magazine*, 16 June 2023, www.Harvardmagazine.com.

4 Huras, "Campus Conversation."

5 Huras, "Campus Conversation."

6   Stephen Holmes, "The Antiliberal Idea," *Routledge Handbook of Illiberalism* (New York: Routledge, 2021), 3–15, 3.
7   Holmes quoting Fritz Stern in *The Failure of Illiberalism: Essays on the Political Culture of Modern Germany* (New York: Knopf, 1971); Holmes, *The Failure of Illiberalism*, 3.

Index

Index

121

UTP insights

BOOKS IN THE SERIES

- David B. MacDonald, *The Sleeping Giant Awakens: Genocide, Indian Residential Schools, and the Challenge of Conciliation*
- Paul W. Gooch, *Course Correction: A Map for the Distracted University*
- Paul T. Phillips, *Truth, Morality, and Meaning in History*
- Stanley R. Barrett, *The Lamb and the Tiger: From Peacekeepers to Peacewarriors in Canada*
- Peter MacKinnon, *University Commons Divided: Exploring Debate and Dissent on Campus*
- Raisa B. Deber, *Treating Health Care: How the System Works and How It Could Work Better*
- Jim Freedman, *A Conviction in Question: The First Trial at the International Criminal Court*
- Christina D. Rosan and Hamil Pearsall, *Growing a Sustainable City? The Question of Urban Agriculture*
- John Joe Schlichtman, Jason Patch, and Marc Lamont Hill, *Gentrifier*
- Robert Chernomas and Ian Hudson, *Economics in the Twenty-First Century: A Critical Perspective*
- Stephen M. Saideman, *Adapting in the Dust: Lessons Learned from Canada's War in Afghanistan*
- Michael R. Marrus, *Lessons of the Holocaust*
- Roland Paris and Taylor Owen (eds.), *The World Won't Wait: Why Canada Needs to Rethink Its International Policies*
- Bessma Momani, *Arab Dawn: Arab Youth and the Demographic Dividend They Will Bring*
- William Watson, *The Inequality Trap: Fighting Capitalism Instead of Poverty*
- Phil Ryan, *After the New Atheist Debate*
- Paul Evans, *Engaging China: Myth, Aspiration, and Strategy in Canadian Policy from Trudeau to Harper*